Being a Buddha
on Broadway

Being a Buddha
on Broadway

Access the Power of Your
Naturally Peaceful Mind

BERTRAM W. SALZMAN

InnerDirections
P U B L I S H I N G

InnerDirections Publishing

INNER DIRECTIONS FOUNDATION
P.O. Box 130070
Carlsbad, California 92013
Tel: 800 545-9118 • 760 599-4075
www.InnerDirections.org

Cover and interior design by Joan Greenblatt
Interior photographs by Bertram W. Salzman

Printed in Canada

ISBN: 1-878019-22-8

Library of Congress Catalog Card Number: 2003115500

Acknowledgments

I owe a special debt of gratitude to several people for their support and encouragement throughout the years. Without them, this book might not have been written. They are:

My wife, Jeannie, who is the love of my life and who, over breakfast, patiently listened to my excited dreams for many years

My parents, Phillip and Emma Salzman

Matthew and Joan Greenblatt of Inner Directions, who recognized the truth expressed through these words

My dear friends Alain, Jean-Michel, and Marie-Bertrande, whose kindness never faltered

Jeannie's parents, Wendell and Ruth Davidson

Ron and Dianne Neuman, Paul Gottlieb, and many others who came through for Jeannie and me when we needed it

"A human being is a part of a whole we call 'universe'—a part limited in time and space. He experiences himself, his thoughts and feelings, as something separated from the rest—a kind of optical delusion of his consciousness. This delusion is a prison; our task must be to free ourselves from it."

—ALBERT EINSTEIN

Table of Contents

Foreword

I first met Bertram W. Salzman when we began to work on a spiritually oriented film that he directed and our organization produced. Before our first meeting, we simply exchanged resumes and talked at length on the phone. What struck me during these conversations was the passion and depth of conviction that Bertram brought to everything he did. *This, I thought, is a man I look forward to meeting.*

Over the years we went on to produce three films together, and worked jointly on several other projects. Wherever we traveled together, I found Bertram to be literally "in love with life," and full of affection toward everyone we met along the way. Whether we were in a pharmacy, supermarket, or just walking through downtown Sonoma, Bertram would invariably bring a special light and love to all those who crossed his path. During our many long conversations, he would often say that once we become free from taking the mind to be oneself, an overflowing love and affection becomes our natural way of living. The natural effervescence of his self-awareness simply manifested itself in this manner.

During one of his meditation classes, Bertram spoke of Carl Jung, who, in his commentary in Evans-Wentz's translation of *The Tibetan Book of Great Liberation*, wrote of "the self-liberating power of the introverted mind." Jung went on to comment that "In the East, where this deeply introverted type of meditation is practiced, there is no difficulty in conceiving of a consciousness without an ego."

Bertram Salzman remarked about this passage:

> Some of the students in class who have practiced this deeply introverted form of meditation understood Jung's point and experienced this liberated consciousness. It represents the transformation from the existing, gross (dualistic) mind to the aspect of mind that is extremely subtle (nondual).

> Because most human beings live primarily in the duality of the gross mind, they are simply unable to imagine this unconventional state and are skeptical of Jung's statement. They might even suggest that he was speaking metaphorically. He wasn't!

If anyone had five minutes and cared to experience the subtle mind, Bertram was always happy to help them taste it. He would often say, "Nirvana is now or never; I discovered this when I was eight."

Bertram has been at this "work" continuously for the last sixty-four years, ever since the moment that a mysterious light poured love into his heart during a period of deep despair. He can be seen around coffee shops in his much-loved Sonoma, asking people to inquire "Who am I?"—"But wait!" he'd exclaim with a raised hand, "don't answer with the mind." He knew that it was the "non-answering" that brought with it a real change in one's consciousness.

This book is his story, as well as a manual of transformative ways by which we can discover the infinite subtle mind, which is always vibrantly alive within every human being.

Matthew Greenblatt
Carlsbad, California

Preface

This book is both a mystery story and a "how to" manual. The "Mystery" is another name for Divine consciousness. The "Manual" represents the fruit of years of investigation, inquiry, and insight into the nature of this Mystery. It is my hope that this book will help the reader find answers to life's most significant questions, such as *Who am I?* and *What is the meaning of my existence?*

The Presence and the Mystery

Sixty-three years ago, when I was eight years old, the Mystery revealed itself to me, and I've been hot on its trail ever since. This event transformed an unhappy boy into a tiny (I was small for my age.), single-minded mystical detective/spiritual seeker. Although at the time I could not have known it (Eight-year-olds are far more interested in baseball than life's mysteries.), in one moment I had been transformed. It was as if the breath of the Divine filled me with its love and awareness. Before this extraordinary event I was a downhearted kid; afterward, my eyes looked upward and inward, even in the midst of childhood tears and travail. From then on, my heart was always light, for I had looked into the face of the Mystery and tasted a peace that "passeth all understanding."

This voyage has been difficult at times, and at other times delightfully blissful. Yet, whatever life has brought my way, the wordless presence has been always at my back, urging me to keep going: "It's there . . . You *know*—you've seen it!" It seems that once one is touched in this manner, there is simply no escape from it.

Many years have passed since that event occurred. Whether in combat in Korea or in ecstatic moments of bliss, this Divine presence (which I affectionately refer to as my "Friend") has always remained with me. This book is not the story of an individual; rather it is a narrative of the Divine as it played out in an individual life.

Before I continue, let me state categorically that I cannot claim any special faculty. I am an ordinary person for whom *seemingly* extraordinary events have occurred. I qualified the previous statement because what *seemed* extraordinary at the time of its occurrence is, in fact, quite ordinary from a transcendent point of view. This event is destined to happen to every human being at some time, for it is our true nature and birthright. Ultimately, each of us is destined to awaken to the living presence of a reality that is greater than ourselves. It is *already* within us; *we need only develop an acute awareness of it in order for it to awaken and flower.* Once awakened, this energy will always be available. So it has been for me.

THE SUBTLE MIND

Throughout this book, I make reference to the subtle mind. This is the aspect of our mind that emerges during periods of true meditation and that represents real transformation. Both the subtle and the gross aspects of mind function similarly, except that in the case of the subtle mind, the generally solid distinctions of content, such as "good and bad," "right and wrong," or "I and you," are rendered extremely subtle. In this manner, although you and I still recognize that we are different people, the previously held sense of separateness no longer exists, allowing the experience of nonduality to arise effortlessly and spontaneously.

References to this way of "seeing" have been expressed in various ways: the subtle mind is Jesus' declaration "I and my Father are one"; it is the quality of "Suchness" contained within the "Buddha Mind"; it is the nondual mind of Advaita Vedanta.

NATURAL PEACE

The most sought-after treasure in the world—even more than wealth and power—is peace of mind. Ironically, this state of peace is something that is *naturally* ours. In fact, it is our birthright! If this is truly the case, why do so many people seek what is already theirs?

After years of meditative inquiry and investigation, I found the reason to be clear: people take the small, mechanical aspect of their mind—the calculating, reasoning, and information-processing portion—to be the whole mind. While this limited aspect of the mind is essential for accomplishing daily activities and providing for our way of life, it is important to realize that it exists within a much greater context: the infinite space of the naturally peaceful mind.

Because the gross aspect of mind is dualistic by nature, it views life through the eyes of a separate, divided self. This limited vision results in division, disharmony, and discord. Over the millennia, social systems evolved that were based on this incomplete vision, and these gave rise to a culture of separation among nationalities, races, religions, and individuals. Our current institutions reflect this indiscriminate outlook, and the self-perpetuating drama of human suffering continues. Even religions, which hold the promise of freedom, have become one of the prime casualties of this limited vision of reality.

A mind that regularly worries about the past and future creates problems at every conceivable turn, even when events are clearly not under its control. Originally created as a reasoning and survival mechanism, the finite instrument we call the gross mind has become our sole measuring point of the infinite cosmos. Continuously living in the world of this chattering mind not only causes mental fatigue, it stops us from seeing the larger context of any given moment. It is only when we step outside of thought that we can see things as they really are. Moreover, the merry-go-round of thought creates an environment of stress, which leads to a state of dis-ease in which illnesses such as hypertension, heart disease, digestive disorders, and psychological imbalances easily occur. Yet there is good news: Although we may not always be able to control conditions and events in our life, we *can* control our responses to them.

The state in which most of us live is like a vast, peaceful desert in which a tiny radio is blaring. Although the peaceful nature of the desert is always present as the background, and is itself unaffected by the noise, the noise appears to be the predominant experience. However, turning off the radio reveals the noise to be nothing more than a surface disturbance. In the same way, if we can shut off the constantly chattering mind, the ever-present peace of the subtle mind will be available to us.

Calling upon your power of attention, the exercises in this book will help to guide you—in an easy and precise manner—in accessing the always-present, naturally peaceful, subtle mind. This is the inherent state of inner peace and tranquility, which is your birthright.

ABOUT THIS BOOK

The book is divided into four sections and is ideally read in chapter order. Each section approaches the subject in a unique manner.

REFLECTIONS OF THE JOURNEY

I've shared a few revelatory incidents of my life that demonstrate how a young boy, faced with the loss of his mother and a subsequently depressed spirit, awakened to the peace and joy of the subtle mind, and thereafter pursued the *source* of this awakening.

TALKS WITH STUDENTS

Making reference to conversations with students who took part in ongoing meditation classes, I have presented a variety of topics in the hope of benefiting a broad number of readers.

POINTERS ON THE WAY

These expressions are meant to convey how this author experiences the world from the perspective of the subtle mind.

ATTENTION EXERCISES

These exercises were originally developed in France, then further refined and tested with my California students. The collection that you'll find here covers the most effective approaches I've found and enables one to quickly move out of the gross mind into the peace of the subtle mind.

Bertram W. Salzman
Sonoma, California

PART ONE

"Why do you weep?
The source is within you
And this whole world is
springing up from it."
—RUMI

Reflections of the Journey

Idecided to write this book when I was eight. The decision was really not made by my adult self, but by that eight-year-old. He had been in deep despair because his mother had died when he was just four, then he had subsequently experienced a significant event that brought him complete and lasting happiness. In an expression of gratitude, he made a promise at that time to a special "Friend"—Divine consciousness—that he would help to heal the world as he had been healed.

I write this at seventy-one, so the work has been developing for many years and has, at last, emerged in its final form. How does one write an introduction to one's life? When I was born, no one handed me pencil and pad and said, "Here, some day you'll be asked to write an introduction, so start taking notes."

I was born in Brooklyn in 1931, but it was several years later that I actually became fully aware of myself on the world stage. For the briefest moment there was darkness, then suddenly the curtain parted and there "I" was—and there was everything else. The world and I had risen in tandem. My mother was at the kitchen stove; my dog, Queeny, was at my side. There was also a subtle presence that welcomed me to Life.

When I was four years old my mother died, and my father was unable to take care of my older sister, my older brother, and me. After I was nearly hit by a car while playing in the street, my sister, Gloria, was sent to live with an aunt while my brother, Marvin, and I were sent to a Jewish orphanage called the Pride of Judea Children's Home. I was four and one-half—old enough to figure out that my life had changed in a big way.

On the morning we arrived at the orphanage, my brother explained to me that our mother was dead and we would never see her again. My heart felt heavy and I became very, very sad. I remember staring down at the ground with tears coming out of my eyes; I kept hearing Marvin say over and over again, "Mama is dead; we won't ever see her again."

FROM THE HEARTS OF BABES

I awoke on my seventh birthday feeling really light, as if something good was going to happen. Maybe someone was going to give me a birthday present; perhaps it was the electric train set I had seen in the window of a toy store. I was just lying there in bed when all of a sudden I began to whisper to myself. It was as if I were repeating the words of someone who was inside of me; it sounded like my voice, only I was older:

You're seven now; you're not a baby anymore.

This was the only thing the voice said. The idea that I was not a baby any more made me feel good, even though I didn't know why.

A few weeks later, during Sabbath services in the temple, the Rabbi was telling our group of kids—though I think he was really looking at me— "When a child loses a parent, God then becomes the parent that child has lost." I didn't really understand what he meant, but the words had considerable impact, and I couldn't forget them.

At about this same time, at Public School 202 in Brooklyn, I had Mrs. Braverman for music appreciation. The class met in the school assembly hall, where Mrs. Braverman taught us to memorize classical pieces by matching word rhymes to the melody. I listened to her but was feeling sad as usual. I stared down at the floor and said to myself, *C'mon already, Mrs. Braverman, let's get it over with.* I was still feeling bad about my mother's death and being sent to the orphan home. Little did I know what was about to happen.

As I sat there in the assembly hall, slumped in my seat, I was staring at a beam of sunlight that shone on the head of the girl just in front of me. I saw that the sun had moved a little bit, and now a bright beam of light was falling across the lap of my corduroy knickers. I bent forward and the sun hit me directly in the face. I leaned back and noticed that rays of the sun were starting to come in through the large windows of the assembly hall. As I continued to watch the light, I began to sense a joyful feeling in my chest that I had never felt before.

Mrs. Braverman continued to crank the handle of the portable RCA Victorola, explaining that the record she was about to play was the "Morning Movement" from *The Peer Gynt Suite* by Edvard Greig. She went on to tell us how Peer Gynt, who lived high in the Alps, would get up every day at dawn to look at the sunrise over the distant peaks. At the right moment, he would raise his arms up to heaven and the valley below would fill with bright rays of golden sunshine, as though Peer Gynt himself had given a command. *How great*, I thought. I really loved the story and began to sing loudly in time with the music along with the other kids:

Morning is breaking and Peer Gynt is waking;
Morning from Peer Gynt by Greig.

I was so happy. I stood up and raised my arms as Peer Gynt did, concentrated on the light shining in from the big windows and began swaying with the music, which filled my head and heart. All of a sudden, the entire assembly hall turned bright; everything and everybody was glowing in a golden light. My head filled with a tangible, vibrating feeling that I could actually hear. It sounded like a million fireflies were in my brain. My whole body was shaking and glowing.

For the first time in my life, I was truly happy and completely peaceful. I looked into the bright light and smiled, and something in that golden light knew how I felt and breathed love back into my heart. I kept singing:

Morning is breaking and Peer Gynt is waking . . .

If you understand, things are just as they are;
if you do not understand, things are just as they are.
—Zen proverb

THE "PRESENCE" RETURNS UNINVITED

A number of years after leaving the orphanage, and having lived in various loveless foster homes for some time, I decided to enlist in the Marines. I was seventeen years old and eager to take on the world as an adult. I had an above-average IQ and had been offered several interesting beginner jobs, several of which I'd been keen to take. However, since the military draft was still active, enlisting seemed the best way for me to avoid being drafted early in a new career. Plus, apartments were scarce and money even scarcer.

World War II had recently ended, and no one considered another war even remotely possible. So what was the harm? The solution seemed clear. To everyone's surprise—especially mine—I enlisted.

Less than two years later, I found myself in a landing craft, storming a seawall in Inchon, Korea. As we approached the shore, bullets and rockets filled the air around us. In the midst of this combat hell, I became frozen as fear literally choked me. I was sure this was the end. At the zenith of this terror, I heard a wordless voice reassuring me: *Be still; it's okay.* Calmness ran through me like a river, engulfing my entire body.

A stillness filled my soul. As we stormed the seawall, events took place as if in slow motion. I climbed the rope ladder and dove over the wall. Peace reigned within. My "Friend" was with me.

*In the attitude of silence the soul finds the path in a clearer light,
and what is elusive and deceptive resolves itself into crystal clearness.*
—Mahatma Gandhi

"IT DON'T MEAN A THING . . ."

After being discharged from military service, I spent several years doing work that I felt was not at all suited to my nature. I quickly discovered that most of the commercial world fell into this category—especially the advertising business. It's not that I had moral or other misgivings about business; in fact, some of it was fun, and some of my coworkers became friends. It's just that the work didn't *feel* natural; it was always a struggle. I couldn't seem to find the rhythm, the "bounce" of the business. As Ella Fitzgerald sings, "It don't mean a thing if it ain't got that swing." I learned early on that I'd never be able to do the "business boogy."

How was I to bring deeper meaning to my daily work? Something a coworker said when I showed him some drawings I'd done in Central Park gave me a clue to the direction my life might be needing to take. After studying my sketches, this commercial artist said, "Now I know why you're unhappy working in business. You're a flower trying to grow in a vegetable garden."

I asked him to explain. He took me to the window, pointed to an interesting-looking five-story building, and said, "There's your garden." He was pointing at the Art Students League of New York, a building that was to become my home for the next three years.

From the first day I set foot in "The League," as it had come to be known, I knew I had found a sort of spiritual home. Art seemed so natural that I felt a warm glow within. The perfume of the Presence lingered in the hallways and classrooms for the entire three years of my attendance. I was happy. This indeed *was* my garden. It was infused with a mysterious beauty that would arrive unexpectedly and silence my mind for days.

One day, while having lunch in the League cafeteria, I mentioned these periods of silence to a friend. It was in the context of a conversation about Zen. This man was a Zen meditator, and I felt comfortable speaking about my "significant event" with him. When I had finished, he smiled, picked up the book sitting next to him, and handed it to me. It was a pocket edition of Herman Hesse's *Siddhartha*.

"Here, read this; it will tell you more than I can about that experience," he said, adding, "What you've been experiencing is what Zen is all about."

Since I was unfamiliar with the principles of Zen, I wasn't sure what he meant. These periods of Silence had come and gone on their own for many years. I had always assumed that this was the way it was for everyone, just as I'd assumed (wrongly, it turns out) that all of the children in Mrs. Braverman's music appreciation class had experienced the "significant event" in the same manner that I had. "After all," I reasoned, "this must be why people listen to music."

As my Buddhist friend and I continued our conversation, I began to hear that familiar inner sound of fireflies that usually preceded the "silence." I thanked the fellow and hurried out, eager to read the book.

Before this meeting I had never spoken in much detail about my "significant event" to anyone, except once—during a particularly strange circumstance. I was driving, and quite flustered because I was stuck in heavy New York traffic and late for an important appointment. The car radio was tuned to the local classical music station. That morning the station began to play the "Morning Movement" of *The Peer Gynt Suite*, which I immediately recognized. I unconsciously began to sing Mrs. Braverman's lyric:

Morning is breaking and Peer Gynt is waking . . .

In a flash, I was hurled back—full color, sound, and emotion—into the middle of the original event at the P. S. 202 assembly hall. Here I'd been experiencing the impatience associated with a big city traffic jam, and all of a sudden I'm transported to the ecstasy of this extraordinary golden light, complete with rhapsodic music.

The shock of this drastic transition was much too much for my nervous system, and I began to weep. I pulled over in front of Saks Fifth Avenue to avoid causing an accident, my tears gushing uncontrollably, and babbled the entire story to my bewildered passenger in an attempt to explain this bizarre behavior. I'm sure he didn't comprehend even a tiny bit of what I told him. Had a cell phone been available at that moment, no doubt he would have dialed 911.

Now I walked down Broadway to Forty-Second Street, crossed Times Square, and headed east toward the main city library, where I planned to spend the afternoon reading *Siddhartha*. As I walked, I studied the face of Siddhartha on the book cover. *So serene*, I thought, and wondered, *But what if he had lived on Broadway?*

I searched my mind for the reason that the "inner fireflies" had suddenly erupted in my brain. It had something to do with that tranquil expression, which seemed achingly familiar. I jogged up the wide steps of the library and entered its peaceful, silent halls, and at that moment I knew what it was. The silence in Siddhartha's expression had begun vibrating within me. His expression had the same quality of silence and peace I'd felt when I had stood, raised my arms toward the light, and sung "Morning is breaking . . . "! The fireflies responded by turning up the volume; they were doing their version of Handel's *Messiah*. I chuckled as the Presence descended upon me.

I read the book my friend had lent me. Hadn't the transformation of Siddhartha come at the moment of his deepest despair, as had mine? The Presence in the light that had smiled at me during Mrs. Braverman's music class many years earlier was the same eternal Presence that Siddhartha had experienced when he studied the glowing net of pearls.

After reading *Siddhartha* for the third time, I took up meditation. From then on, I stayed with the practice in one form or another—even after leaving art school, and while pursuing the demanding career of a filmmaker. During those times, I always felt that familiar silence. It has never abandoned me.

There's a joke about an old New York street fiddler who's approached by a tourist and asked,
"How do I get to Carnegie Hall?"
"Practice," the fiddler replies.

ELECTRICITY MADE SIMPLE

When my G. I. Bill of Rights ran out in 1960, so did my art school tuition payments.

I tried working in a frame shop for a while, but the hours were long and the pay short. So, when I was approached by an ex-student friend with the offer of a temporary gofer/lighting position on a low-budget industrial film, I grabbed it. The friend asked me if I knew a little about electricity and I said "yes," although I knew nothing.

"Good," he responded, "because you'll be working with heavy movie lights." He took me to the film equipment rental company and pointed out the lighting equipment that we would be using, rattling off some technical specs about them. I was totally confused and was about to tell my friend to hire someone else, but he already suspected that I was in over my head and suggested that I spend some time familiarizing myself with the equipment.

When he left, I stood there, lost. I asked John Henry, a young man who worked at the film equipment company, if he could help me. He knew from the rental contract when the job was to begin, and suggested, "You've got six days, and I'll be working nights, when it's slow. Come in around six every evening, and in a few days I'll teach you what you need to know to get started—all for only twenty bucks." He smiled and added, "Meanwhile, go to a secondhand bookstore, buy a copy of *Electricity Made Simple*, and read it through three times."

For nearly four hours every evening, John Henry and I pored through *Electricity Made Simple*. We also set up and took down just about every movie light in the shop about ten times. I was later to follow the same procedure with *Motion Picture Photography Made Simple*, after I was offered a job as assistant cameraman.

And that's the way my movie career proceeded. I moved through every job on the set: Lighting, Camera, Sound, Assistant Director, and finally Writer-Director-Producer. I learned each craft on the job with the help of friends and the "made simple" books, which were quite useful because of the clear, systematic manner in which the subjects were addressed. It was easy to cut through the chaff and get to the heart of a particular subject without wasting a lot of time.

For me, the "made simple" books became a practical and efficient way of getting a very inexpensive education. I was a high school dropout, yet—between these books and some caring friends who were my professors at the New York school of "You're on your own, buddy"—I managed to "graduate" with honors.

FINDING CALM AMID CHAOS

My need to remain composed in the face of the inherent chaos of the entertainment industry proved a daily challenge. During the 1970s, while working on a six-month contract for NBC, I wrote and directed a number of dramas about the involvement of children in the Revolutionary War. I remember how, on the first day of work, two opposing camps of staffers in production departments approached me, each warning me of the other camp's duplicity and betrayal tactics. I had been forewarned that this might happen, so I brought my prior years of practice into play and managed to steer my way through the rocky shoals for the duration of my contract.

I survived the ordeal because of my ability to be Buddha-like in my approach to both camps. The compassionate understanding of each person's life was a natural quality found in the inner silence of my practice. It was this compassionate silence that gave me the ability to keep a serene distance. Each side assumed that I loved them the most, and in fact I did.

On another occasion, when I complained about the quality of the music NBC created for the series, I was called into a vice president's office and warned that any further complaining would cost me my job. This man had hired me because he liked my work, but complaining about quality on the set was a "no-no," as he put it.

I asked him if quality was important to him, and he responded in the affirmative, but added that corporate profits were even more important. I saw that he was frightened and didn't want to go over budget, which was also a "no-no." I realized that budget overruns could cost him his job, so I smiled and said, "I understand." He was so relieved at having avoided conflict that he put an arm around my shoulder and offered to take me to lunch. I accepted, but never accepted work from NBC again. This prevailing attitude in the entertainment industry of profits over quality was a contributing factor in my choosing early retirement.

One might ask why, since I had this transformation at age eight, I would not at all times be a Buddha on Broadway. I was . . . *inwardly*! Despite the daily frenzy and uncertainty of the entertainment industry, I was able to remain detached. My empty consciousness was like a hollow reed that at times became momentarily submerged by the torrent of a mad, rushing river, but quickly resurfaced to flow once again toward its ultimate destination.

Over the years, I established a reputation as a filmmaker and wrote, directed, and produced children's educational films for television. For a number of these films, I managed to win prestigious awards. In 1976, after winning an Academy Award for "Best Live Action Short Film" (*Angel and Big Joe*), I felt I had achieved enough in the outer world and decided to turn my full attention inward and address the life of the soul.

The search to discover my true identity had nagged me even in the middle of directing a film. The question *Who am I?* was with me when I went to sleep at night and when I awoke the next morning. I fervently needed a change in lifestyle that would reduce outward distractions while giving me an opportunity to settle deeply within myself. I decided on early retirement in order to have time to go more deeply into meditation, an aspect of my life that had long been my central focus. My wife, Jeannie, and I had visited France many years before and we loved the bucolic countryside. We decided to buy a small farmhouse in the Loire Valley.

SATORI AT LUNCH

One morning, at the time Jeannie and I were considering moving to France for a minimum of five years, a close friend and associate (a film producer) argued with me against the move. He said my career was arcing upward and that a five-year interruption would be disastrous. No one would remember me when I returned, he insisted. This associate was making a sound point, given the transient nature of our business.

Yet I told him that, recently, a deep need had arisen in me—with almost uncontrollable urgency—that required that I have the space and freedom to explore my personal universe. I wanted to go back to painting and spend longer periods in meditation. I admitted that I was able to do some of these things while still actively writing and directing, but my professional life was making increasing demands on my time, which in turn had begun to limit my activities in these areas. I was beginning to feel like a spiritual dilettante. In France, I would have the opportunity to read lots of Eastern philosophy and perhaps do some writing on the subject of spirituality.

"But what about your *career?*" he exclaimed.

Suddenly, from out of nowhere, I heard myself respond loudly as I pounded on his desk, "My whole life is my career, not just making films! I want to be as creative with *everything* in my life as I have been with my filmmaking." And with those words there came a great calm and clarity on the subject. It was an epiphany that answered most of my lingering questions concerning the move. I say "most" because an insight that was to come later that day really cleared all lingering doubts.

A filmmaker friend who'd inherited large sums of money from his family had just won his second Oscar for a magnificent live-action nature short film. He asked me to lunch to celebrate, and insisted on going to a fine restaurant known for its extremely expensive hamburgers.

In fact, the hamburgers were superb. I congratulated my friend on his second Oscar and joked that, since I only had one, he was ahead of me in the race to be the man with the most Oscars. He fell silent for a while and then responded thoughtfully, "No, in a way you're ahead, Bert. You see, I've personally financed every film I've done. No producer has ever believed enough in my films to finance them. On the other hand, producers seem to be eager to finance all of your scripts."

I was taken aback by his statement. This friend was wealthy beyond all imagination yet envious of me, who just about got by. The irony of this was astounding. Here I was, debating a move that would give me personal freedom but preclude the possibility of my ever earning substantially more than I ever had. It would also effectively eliminate any ability to accumulate money for retirement.

I thought of my many years of arduous struggle as I'd tried to sell my projects. If I'd had his "dough," I would have been happy to finance my own films. I watched as my friend bit into his scrumptious hamburger and thought of universal justice, and of how, with all of his money, he couldn't under any circumstances enjoy his hamburger any more than I did mine.

For the sake of a vague notion of security in some distant future, it was just not worth my freedom to continue to pursue another Oscar or riches of any kind. That hamburger could never taste any better— no matter how much money or success I accumulated. So what was the point of wasting my life on ego gratification or material gain? It just wasn't worth it! Jeannie and I would get along just fine in our old age—unless I lived with the regret that I had failed to seize the moment of securing my freedom.

At that moment, in the middle of that fancy New York restaurant, something an Eastern sage had once said crossed my mind: *They that are content are the richest on earth and in heaven, for they need nothing.*

Two weeks later, Jeannie and I left for what was to be nearly a ten-year stay in France. There the food was superb—even more marvelous than the food in that overpriced hamburger joint. And a lot cheaper.

For a few brief moments, when we'd first made our decision, Jeannie and I had lain in bed talking about whether we'd chosen the right path. Apart from those short discussions, we never regretted our choice and never looked back. In the end, I never really felt it was my choice to make anyway; it has always been the choice of my "Friend." I've just followed orders.

*To penetrate into the essence of all being and significance, and to release
the fragrance of that inner attainment for the guidance and benefit of others,
by expressing in the world of forms—truth, love, purity, and beauty—this
is the sole game that has any intrinsic and absolute worth. All other incidents
and attainments can, in themselves, have no lasting importance.*
—Meher Baba

OVER THERE

In 1982, at the age of fifty, following a twenty-two year career in film
and television, I retired to a small farmhouse in the Loire Valley, in
central France. Jeannie created a flower garden that a visitor from
New York described as "to die for." I painted, studied, meditated,
and began creating the exercises that were to eventually become
part of this book—first by using myself as a guinea pig and then by
experimenting on unsuspecting guests:

> **Me:** What happens when you put your full attention in the
> space two feet in front of your body?
> **Guest:** Okay . . . whew . . . hey, what did you do?
> **Me:** I did nothing; you just shifted your attention from the
> world of thought to the physical universe, and you woke up
> to your potential.

What was encouraging was that the results of these Attention
Exercises were uniform. Each shift of attention away from thought
brought with it a sense of relief—an ending of tension and stress.
Maybe, I surmised, this could work as a sort of calming therapy.

Over the next several years, I continued to create similar
Attention Exercises, and each one again seemed to achieve uniform

results as described above. My reading of J. Krishnamurti—especially his dialogues with the noted physicist Dr. David Bohm, and the brief but illuminating chats I later had with both of them—confirmed what I had learned in my experiments. The practice of choiceless awareness, which Krishnamurti recommended, brought an ending to thought during those periods.

This made sense to me because, if anything, thought is a choice-making "machine." When there is no work for this machine to do—no choices available to make—it just shuts down and waits for another choice to come along. If choiceless awareness is continued with a certain vigor, the conditioned movement that propels uncontrolled thought (mind chatter) may in some way atrophy, resulting in a fundamental change to the conditioned mind. Thought would still be available when it was needed for an appropriate purpose, such as building a house or changing a flat tire, but it would fall silent when not needed.

Remarkably, it was there in that small village that I met someone who was to introduce me to this extraordinary man and teacher, J. Krishnamurti. About a year after Jeannie and I moved to our French farmhouse, I first met Krishnamurti (who was affectionately addressed as Krishnaji) while attending a talk at his school in Brockwood Park, England, to which I had been invited by a mutual friend, JMB, who lived with his family just outside our village.

I was invited to join Krishnaji at lunch, where I took the opportunity to ask him what was the best way to benefit from his teaching. "Go into it, Mr. Salzman, seriously, as though your life depended on it . . . it does, you know. Don't be a dilettante."

I told him about my farmhouse in France and my early retirement. "Well, then you have leisure, and one definition of leisure is 'time for study.' So get to it!" I was motivated by these words, and spent the next six months reading all of Krishnaji's books and listening to many hours of his talks on video and audiotape.

WORDSWORTH'S CHILD

By B. W. Salzman

The child is the father of the man said he
(And the mother of the woman as well)
The boy first free then led to hell
The girl to serving tea

The child now weeps within its mind
Its sorrow numbs its soul
Lost orphan of the whole
Deep grief of humankind

How long can innocents' child endure
Lone lightless nights unquelled
Times mirthless joyless spell
Unloved unloving spore?

How did this gracious babe of spring
Fatherless become by fall

Now ungraced of all
With voice that dare not sing?

But cannot yet a stifled man
Be father-child again
Bewildered as was then
When swift in fields he ran?

And cannot yet a stunted soul
Be mother-child once more
Alive at magic's door
Enchanted by the whole?

Or is it fixed within the seed this hell
This sorrowed fruit to be
Plucked from Eden's tree
Watered from Satan's well?

Yet can one when awakened see
Its parent as virtue's child
Its nature undefiled
Unframed, unformed, and free?

OH, THE SORROW

Christine had come to France with Emily, a film producer with whom
I'd worked for many years. Emily had visited us several times before,
so when she telephoned from New York to invite us to dinner at our
mutually favorite restaurant in a nearby village, we gladly accepted.

Both Emily and Christine were divorced, and both would turn fifty on the same day in the following week. They wanted to visit us and celebrate the occasion with Jeannie and me. At one time, Emily had owned a house in our village. She hinted during her telephone call that Christine might also be interested in buying a house in this village, and would we keep our eyes open for something suitable. She reminded me that both she and Christine had graduated cum laude from an Ivy League women's college, and that if I had seen or read Mary McCarthy's *The Group* I would have some idea of Christine's taste.

I had always suspected that Emily and her classmates might very well have served as models for the characters in *The Group*: They were smart, sassy, ambitious, and certain of their superiority. These women insisted that they would have perfect husbands, perfect careers, and perfect loving children. This was for sure, and the world had no say in it! Of course, it didn't turn out that way. Emily and Christine came to France to celebrate their fiftieth birthdays with former business colleagues. Something seemed amiss. Where were their families on this very special occasion? I felt a pang of sadness as I wondered about it.

After their arrival, we spent several busy days searching for a house for Christine but could not find anything suitable. Christine became increasingly desperate as the hours passed. Finally, she had only one more day, and after seeing how Jeannie and I lived, she too wanted—*needed*—to have a "cozy farmhouse" in the Loire Valley. Everything in her life, she had confessed earlier, was meaningless, and she felt *cheated*! The promised life she had dreamed of in her youth turned out to be an illusion—a farce of mammoth proportions. She had suffered "the terrible twos": two bad marriages, two indifferent children, and two horrible jobs from which she had either walked out or been fired. To top it all, her lover of two years had recently confessed that he'd fallen in love with another woman.

When it became apparent that she wasn't going to find anything, at least not on this trip, Christine walked out into the garden of the last house on the agent's list, leaned against a tree, and began to weep in frustration. Great heaving sobs engulfed her.

As I saw the tears falling from Christine's cheeks, a thick gray sadness suddenly overwhelmed me. I could feel her hurt, her pain. Sadness arose within me for all of those whose lives had slipped from the joy and hope of childhood to the sorrow of a lonely, disappointing, adulthood. *And so quickly!* I felt I needed a thousand hearts in which to contain the compassion I felt for this tortured soul. I thought of Siddhartha gazing at the net of pearls and realizing that all of life was one connected unity. I saw that Christine's sorrow was my sorrow. In fact, I *was* Christine. Hadn't I wept this way so long ago at the orphanage when my brother said to me, "We'll never see Mama again"?

I felt an urgent sense that I had to do something, *anything* to end the seemingly unending despair of the human heart. Hadn't I been blessed, miraculously touched, graced, and reborn out of darkness into light? Without that miraculous event, my life might also have turned out to be one of insane sadness. I felt profound gratitude, and with it a strong sense of obligation. I knew my "Friend" had had a hand in all of this and was now calling in my markers. If that blessing had been bestowed on me, then why not on someone like Christine? Why not on all the Christines of the world, or at least some of them? Or maybe just *one* of them?

It was then that I decided to write this book. It would be a "how to" type of book, a manual of ways that people might use to discover their own happiness. I had been given so much; it was time for me to pay it forward. If I could be an instrument to help someone awaken from the apparent darkness, maybe it would be the same as saving the entire world.

I had come to live in France to have the time and space to write a book that would help human beings awaken, just as I had awakened at age eight. The following day, I began to write a book that I hoped would help at least *one* person awaken (an easier and more modest goal, or so I thought at the time). Although most people never seemed to care or understand what I was up to, I'd had a lot of fun reading what seemed like hundreds of books written by others who may have been similarly touched. The only research needed might already be embedded in the curious facts of my life. And didn't I have my "Friend," who was always ready to straighten me out in the event I got too self-assured?

A man does not seek to see himself in running water, but in still water. For only what is itself still can impart stillness to others.
—Chuang Tzu

A SINGLE INQUIRY
The Presence that I speak of is like space; it remains and is never absent, though at times it may appear to be so. For example, right at

this moment your attention is on this page, or—if your attention is highly focused—on just one word in this sentence. For you in this very moment (because of your focused attention), your car has no existence, nor does your kitchen, nor even the ordinary sense of yourself. Even the world doesn't appear to exist in its gross form. Both you and the world have become extremely subtle, and the only apparent existent reality is that one word on which you have focused your attention.

This is how attention (focused awareness) creates the immediate world each moment. In fact, "now" is really only the power of attention, which creates an *apparent* "now." When attention goes to a memory of the past or projects a concept into the future, this apparent "now" vanishes like your car. Not so the attention. It continues, but may presently be focused on an image of the past or future. Because attention is not created by thought, it exists outside of the dimension called "time." It is timeless, as is space, and therefore "never not here." After all, where else could space be? Where could it go?

As the great sage Ramana Maharshi lay dying, he was implored by his followers not to leave them. He replied, "Where can I go? I am here." Ramana knew that his real nature was timeless awareness. And, as with space, there was no other place to go.

Six months after my initial talk with Krishnamurti, I made a breakthrough in understanding his essential teaching. Following this breakthrough, I was inwardly empty and silent for a number of days. Not long after, Krishnaji came to France on a vacation, to stay at a chateau near our village. I looked forward to our second meeting, wanting to tell him of my insight. You might say that Bert wanted a bit of stroking, although at the time I didn't see this.

When we did meet again, Krishnamurti was to ask me (in an exchange that lasted no more than five minutes) a question that would thereafter give me a way to establish—with certainty—the truth of anything I "knew."

Jeannie prepared a sumptuous Indian vegetarian lunch for Krishnaji at the home of our mutual friend, JMB. After a second portion of fruit compote dessert, Krishnaji rose and headed for the sitting room. I had anticipated this and rose to join him.

He looked over and asked, smiling, "Well, have you gone into the teaching as you planned?"

I was pleased that he remembered our last meeting. "Yes, and with remarkable results," I replied.

"Tell me," he said.

I told him of my in-depth studies and my subsequent insight into his basic teaching.

"And what, Mr. Salzman, do you suggest that is?" he inquired.

"Freedom comes with the ending of the known," I replied. I then went on to tell him of the experience of emptiness that had accompanied this insight.

But before I could go on, he held up his hand and asked, "Tell me, Mr. Salzman, is the experience of that silence alive *now*? Or are you telling me this from memory about an event of the past, which is thought, and so there is no freedom from the known at this very moment. What good is a memorized understanding of the teaching in your life today?"

The question was a shocker. Krishnaji had correctly seen that the remarkable insight I was so passionately recalling was no longer alive *now*! I was relating an intellectual fact, and he was reminding me of this with his question. I suddenly saw what I was doing, and this realization emptied my mind. I was literally stunned. I stuttered something like, "Oh yes . . . wow. I see."

Krishnamurti smiled and turned to walk on, but then turned back and said softly, so the others wouldn't hear, "You know, Mr. Salzman, life is now or never. So drop all we've spoken about here, as it has already become part of the past."

He then walked into the sitting room, where he was met by our hostess. In the midst of all this, I suddenly recalled the words of a poem by William Blake that expressed in poetry what Krishnaji had just taught me with that one inquiry.

> He who bends to himself a joy
> Does the winged life destroy;
> But he who kisses the joy as it flies
> Lives in eternity's sunrise.
> —William Blake

A Second Significant Event

Words, words, words. My career as a writer-director of films required that I be able to use language. I depended on words to describe the action and events ascribed to the characters in my scripts. Each day, my consciousness was filled with words. I engaged in all this "wording" because my livelihood depended upon it, but I always felt uncomfortable being dependent upon words. I felt like a word junky who was living in an unreal world, much in the way I imagine an opium smoker might feel while smoking a pipe full of the drug.

I remember a period in the late sixties, in New York, when people practically stopped offering alcohol at parties. Marijuana had become the stimulant of choice. I decided to see what all the fuss was about, and tried it on several occasions. During these occurrences I lost clarity; an uncomfortable heaviness and unawareness descended that would remain for many hours. This feeling was vaguely familiar. I recognized it as something I had experienced before, and knew that it was also something to be avoided. Suddenly, I realized that this feeling was similar to the state of consciousness I'd experienced just after my mother died—a feeling that remained until my music-class epiphany freed me and filled me with that extraordinary light.

I stopped using marijuana, and the discomfort disappeared. But I couldn't quit using my daily ration of "the word" drug. Yes, drug. Why? While words are indispensable to communication, my dependence on them and heavy overuse had created a fog in my consciousness similar to that caused by marijuana. I asked myself *Why is this?* Before long I would get the answer.

In France, I was reading various spiritual works—among them a book by Ludwig Wittgenstein, the great philosophical linguist. Wittgenstein argued that words can be dangerous, since they have the ability to create a false reality. Words are, in fact, only symbols that represent *actual* things and events. Yet, think of the solid reality that words have come to possess—as if they *were* reality.

For example, look at the words "America, France, Asia, Christian, man, woman, tree." How solid and alive these words seem to be. They are almost as experiencable as the things they represent. (I say "almost" because one can never eat the word "apple.")

I realized that the symbol-word separates, then creates a solid, unbridgeable gap between oneself and the objects of existence ("what is")—the unnamed world that exists prior to and independent of the names we ascribe to it. This occurrence seemed to account for the feeling of a dark, slightly out-of-focus reality. Was it truly the gap between the name and the actual reality of the object itself that creates this sense of separation?

Since I'd been living in France, the word "France" had acquired a certain solid reality for me; I lived in *France*. When I looked out through the studio window, all that I observed was France. Then it hit me. I heard the word "wrong" echo in my head. I had said that all I observed was France. This was an error; I should have said that what I observed was what I observed, and what I observed happened to be *named* "France." I wondered then what the experience of this observation would be if the *word* "France" didn't exist. Would my reality, my sense of self and place, change?

I found a small slate, wrote the word "France," and studied it for a period of several minutes until the word took on a solid reality. Next I took a wet cloth and wiped the slate clean in one movement. When the word vanished, I was amazed to discover that France had also vanished along with its name! What remained was a vast, unnamed space containing unnamed objects. "France" had completely disappeared and could not be found, either inwardly or outwardly.

I wondered, *If France could disappear so easily, what about Bertram W. Salzman?* I took up the slate again, wrote my name on it, then wiped it clean. There was a sudden shift in my psychological center: Bertram W. Salzman had also vanished. Disappeared! What remained was an extremely subtle, centerless, and egoless "me." I was weightless and transparent, timeless and fearless. I looked out through the window at the village scene where I had always been the "subject," with people or things as objects. Now, with this sudden shift, both the world and I had become objects. The complete psychological structure associated with my personality—the very underpinnings of my identity—had dissolved. In essence, the individual personality known as Bertram W. Salzman had died instantly upon being unnamed, and an all-pervading nature—the only real thing about him—had arisen to take his place. This truly was death and resurrection!

What remained was a transparent void, an emptiness, which became instantly filled with the "things" of this world. With the ending of "me," these things came alive both within and without. In fact, "within" and "without" were experienced as just one movement, with all of existence seemingly dying and flowering again in one timeless moment. Everything was in the sharpest focus; the colors and shapes of objects were beyond vivid, and more real and beautiful than I had ever previously experienced them to be. The splendor of it was beyond expression. The trees outside the window appeared animate. I felt that they were aware of my presence and would have spoken had they had the ability to do so. I said hello to them and knew that they heard me. They responded in their own way.

I could never look at those trees again and think of them as just trees. In "unnaming" them and myself, I had been freed! They rushed fully alive into my void-like consciousness. I became the world and the world became me. I saw clearly that separation is an illusion, that "I," as a separate entity, was a work of fiction. Tears filled my eyes. I was awake!

That day, I was freed from the prison of words—an inner prison that had separated me from the world. I had now closed the mental gap between life and myself, and all was full of light. Afterward, I would never rely on words when attempting to know Reality. This insight had the effect of clearing away a final barrier to the direct experience of Truth. As a result, I always ask my students to learn to see and listen, and to refrain from conceptualizing about what they experience.

Later, while driving with Jeannie through the lovely French countryside, I was full of the substance of life. To say that I loved the pastures, the farms, and the sky would be incorrect. I simply *was* all of it. The intimacy was profound. We intermingled—not as form but vibrationally, with forms endlessly dissolving and then flowing one into the other as vibrational waves, becoming distinct material entities only to dissolve once again. All this took place in timelessness. I realized that the entire human life span occurs in this same infinitesimally brief duration, and that when this life vibration forms as a physical body, it forgoes its eternal nature in order to become form. As we drove, I looked over at Jeannie and asked her to unname France. She did so, smiled, and said, "Wow."

What gives that brief moment its *apparent* sense of continuity and time is the fixing of events and objects with words—naming them. It is the act of unnaming that unfixes form, allowing it to revert to its eternal, flow-like, vibrational nature. All of the longing for love present in the human heart is really a deep yearning to move from form to the unity of reality called Life. This is our true nature; it is who and what we really are.

But why, I wondered, did infinite life create—then *apparently* limit—itself as form? I waited silently. A few minutes later, the reply rushed into my brain: *In order to know itself!* Life, being one, had no other way to know its own existence, just as an eye has no way of seeing itself without a mirror. The human mind, I suddenly realized, is the mirror in which life can reflect upon itself. At that moment, I saw that the entire purpose of human existence is to facilitate the awakening of life to itself as eternal consciousness.

Suffering, which is due to an unconscious sense of separation, will end only with the direct experience of Reality. The appropriate teaching, I realized, must dissolve the gross mind's conditioning, which has kept people believing that they are only the physical form. They have to actually *experience* an "unfixing" of form. This would require experiencing it directly, which would result in the psychological death of the ego.

Although the initial response to this experience on the part of my students was relief, I soon found that, in many cases, it also caused fear. As soon as the ego-dominated gross mind returned, so did the ego's fear of death. I needed to convince the students that, if they continued, the solid ego-sense would eventually be replaced by the more loving, nonviolent, subtle mind. Once the students began to experience the subtle mind more regularly, I hoped that they would be reassured of this approach through their own experience. The gross mind is a tough customer—it has tremendous momentum and influence on human consciousness, and will yield only when it faces the much stronger force of focused attention, whose power comes directly from the unlimited Source. The next day, I began to modify the Attention Exercises so that they would accomplish this unfixing of spirit from form and would replace the gross mind with the naturally peaceful subtle mind.

The question remained: Was it possible to use my experience as a "pointer" to indicate to others what I had discovered? I hoped that those who truly seek freedom would take this information, look for themselves, and discover that the freedom they seek is *already* within them; that it is only a matter of turning the attention inward to discover this.

It was the stark reality of this personal experience of transformation that fueled the possibility of transformation in others and would energize the continued pursuit of a deep and sustained inquiry. At times the work seemed unproductive, but I realized I had no say in this endeavor. My "Friend" informed me many times that it was "payback" time. I would never complain, for, to tell the truth, even if I had a choice in the matter I wouldn't have it any other way.

Eventually, there came a time when I asked myself, *Where do I start in developing a way to help people acquire firsthand experience of their natural state of inner peace?* The clear and logical response was, "Start with myself." All else would be hearsay and partial truth. How would this actually come about, and what would facilitate it? I certainly couldn't take the entire world back to Mrs. Braverman's class to replay the whole scene.

I realized that the first step needed was a clearing of one's existing belief system. After all, for me it had been this very belief system that had held within it the sorrow of my mother's death. When the previous belief system had ceased to function, a new and much more subtle mind had arisen by itself. The experience of this subtle mind had brought with it a much more expansive, universal sense of myself and the world. The result was a profound sense of joy and affection for all of life.

I also found that human beings don't need to be in a state of despair and deep introversion in order to come to this transformative experience. This is available to all through the practice of deep self-inquiry—the turning of the mind back to its own source. When the inquiry *Who am I?* takes place, and the mind is asked not to provide an answer—yet attention is held on the question—the source of this attention responds by removing the limited boundary of thought and reveals our unlimited and boundless nature. I've tested this approach in my own life and found that this inquiry, when seriously practiced, will bring about the intended results *each and every time.* I've also used this as the fundamental approach in our meditation classes and found it to be uniformly transformative. It confirms something I heard Krishnamurti say in his talks: "Truth comes with the ending of the false."

Although the transformation experienced by my students during class was impermanent, it experientially proved the existence of the infinite subtle mind. Due to conditioning, the gross mind would return. However, upon further investigation I discovered that, with brief, intense periods of inquiry, the gross mind could be made to cease functioning in its fragmented and endlessly chattering manner.

Just as the silent space of the desert remains, although it *appears* to vanish in the midst of noise, similarly, the subtle mind—like a vibrant musical tone—is an ever-present background, even amid the noise of disturbing, compulsive thought.

When needed, technical thought will automatically be available for useful mundane tasks, while at other times it will remain silent.

One day, I realized upon waking that, to pursue and share the truth of this inquiry with others, a wider venue than my little village was necessary. During the last few years in France, I had created a manual of Attention Exercises. If they were to be useful as a therapeutic tool, as I had envisioned, I needed to do more work. For this reason, and the fact that Jeannie's parents were aging and she wanted to live closer to them, we decided it was time to return to the States.

We kept the house in France and still visit our many friends there to this day.

CALIFORNIA

It was now 1991. With some help from our friends Ron and Diane, Jeannie and I were able to find a modest house in Northern California.

My hope was to further refine the exercises I'd developed during the 1980s in France. For several years I experimented on myself, and also on unsuspecting patrons at a favorite coffeehouse, with questions such as: "What if you knew absolutely nothing? Please don't respond; just wait and ponder the question for two minutes."

The results were amazing. After the two-minute wait, people invariably responded in astonishment, "Bert, you have blown my mind." I explained that it was their complete attention to the question that had actually done this.

I soon formed a meditation class at the local community center and continued to develop the exercises. Although many students realized I was teaching a novel form of meditation, several of the experienced meditators sensed that there might be something else going on. Of course, they were right. However, if I had told them that I was trying to go beyond traditional forms of meditation, they might not have signed up for the course.

They all stayed because what was being taught seemed to allow them to go deeper into meditation, and more quickly. For my part, I probably gained more in the way of deep, sustained silence than they did. Each week I prepared a class outline, and often included a short essay on the philosophical and spiritual grounding for that day's class. This approach forced me to look even more profoundly into the particular exercise we would be doing and to practice and test it as well. I'm sure that this approach deepened the effects of my original "significant event," which had brought me out of darkness into a happier, more peaceful existence.

I finally completed the manual of Attention Exercises then put the manuscript away for a while. About a year later, I took it out to review it and left it on the coffee table. A visiting friend who is a book publisher commented that he was looking for a very simple book of genuine exercises that would take one into the meditative state. I pointed to the manuscript on the coffee table and told him that the book, a manual of brief meditation exercises meant to quiet the mind, was ready. All that was needed was some additional material to give the exercises the proper context. Upon reading the manual, my friend decided to publish the book.

TOTAL FREEDOM

Several days after that conversation with my publisher, I searched through some personal notes I had made in France and came across the following draft of a letter I'd written to a friend but never sent.

Dear A.,

One day, during a casual conversation with a friend, I heard myself use the expression "Total Freedom." This was curious because I had not used these words for many years. At one time, I made use of them casually and somewhat superficially, without regard to what the words truly implied. At other times, I deeply wondered what the actual *experience* of Total

Freedom would feel like. I didn't know then that I would soon discover what this state actually was.

Not long after speaking with my friend, an echo of the phrase "Total Freedom" began to vibrate within my consciousness, along with a nonspecific sense of elation. In the past, whenever this type of vibrating elation occurred, it usually meant something special was going to happen—as it had on the morning of my seventh birthday. This experience went on for months.

One night, I awoke in the early dawn to find my body shaking and vibrating. I knew that something extraordinary was about to happen. Getting out of bed quietly so as not to awaken Jeannie, I went into the kitchen. I was not exactly sure what to do, so I got a pad and pencil, sat down, and waited silently. One half hour passed before it occurred to me that this might have something to do with the notion of Total Freedom that had seemed to possess me lately. With this thought, I suddenly began writing furiously:

> Freedom is always total. Partial freedom, which is anything less than total freedom, is not true freedom. Freedom is not related to structure. Form, whether psychological or physical, must always have a structure, which is necessary to sustain human life. The human body is a physical structure that is maintained psychologically.
>
> A human being can never be completely free of structure. There can be more structure or less structure, but there can never be a complete absence of structure. Because Total Freedom means to be totally free of

structure, it represents the death of the individual. Total
Freedom from structure is death.

With that sentence, I died! Life completely disappeared.
The structure of my entire psychological consciousness
vanished. I'm not sure how long this period lasted; probably
no more than a few minutes, but it might just as well have
been a few thousand years. For that entire period, there was
a gap of utter nothingness.

As the gap closed, the first thing that entered my
consciousness was the sound of my neighbor's rooster
crowing. When I heard it, joy rushed through every cell in
my body. I remember thinking, *So that's it. It's okay; I don't*
mind a little structure. I don't need to be totally free just now.

I loved my neighbor's rooster. His call had awakened
me from death. Later, as I crawled back into bed, Jeannie,
half asleep, muttered, "What's happening?" I answered, "I
died!" She took my hand, smiled, and fell back to sleep.

Love,
Bert

For some time afterward, the following question continued to
arise: What actually had died that night? I knew that, in that
interlude, every vestige of my consciousness had vanished. Gone. In
one instant, nonbeing had replaced being! What had remained was
absence. In that experience, even the subtle center, which had
continued after my most recent previous experience, had disappeared.
It became clear that all of the notions that contributed to my sense
of being Bertram W. Salzman had died.

Immediately upon the occupation of my mind by the silent cosmos, the bogus personality of Bertram had vacated. Because there never really was an individual who existed in the first place, whatever had happened was simply an activity of the infinite. Individual transformation seemed to be but an illusory movement of the cosmos, an eternal transformation that takes place everywhere and in every moment.

Was I now a true Buddha on Broadway? If so, did it really matter within this context? It now seemed that individual transformation was not the end-game.

I had often practiced self-inquiry by asking the question *Who am I?* (then waiting silently—never accepting an answer from thought). Through this inquiry, I never uncovered who I was; rather, the inquiry stripped away the illusion of who I was not.

Since Truth, by its very nature, has the imperative of being truthful, when the limited truth of thought cannot respond to this inquiry, absolute Truth then must! It discloses itself as the truth of an *absence* of a separate, individual self. In light of this, I've remained uncertain as to "who" or what actually died that night. What pulsates in its stead is a silent, all-encompassing *absentness.*

Although I refer to certain occurrences in my life as "significant events," these events exist out of time and, therefore, do not represent any specific "point" at which I can say a transformation of my consciousness occurred. These insights and openings continue to arise on an ongoing basis. The journey is never really complete, for our lives represent only tiny movements in the ever-expanding flow of consciousness.

My lifelong search has revealed that the truth of our ultimate destiny lies dormant within us. Yet, like seeds that contain the knowledge of their ultimate flowering, we remain unaware of this knowledge. To flourish, our inner seed must be nourished with spiritual light. This light is conveyed through the energy of our attention, which flows and nurtures our souls. Its fount is the silent, eternal Source of all life, which unveils itself only in the absence of nontruth—at a time when the mind is completely still.

It seems to me that our desperate search for Truth is no more than the involuntary inner stirrings of a predestined spiritual awakening.

PART TWO

"All of the vexations and anxieties of
life are due to our failure to sink into
our own center and then to
rise out of it on to the plane of
nondistinction where the problems
at once disappear."
—WHAT IS ZEN? BY D. T. SUZUKI

Talks with Students

In workshops and conversations through the years, I've been asked a variety of questions about the nature of meditation and spiritual attainment. During discussions such as these, responses to each question would flow effortlessly. I've selected the following questions and answers to present a good representation of the most typical and essential topics.

THE PURPOSE OF LIFE

Questioner: *I've tried many methods to achieve happiness, but none of them have been successful. What should I do to get rid of my personal problems and become truly happy?*

B. W. Salzman: As long as you identify with the gross mind you may never get rid of problems or the lingering feeling of unhappiness. The gross mind *itself* is the problem. Egocentric thinking will always clash with all of the other apparent egocentric gross minds you come into contact with, and conflict will be the result.

The solution to solving all problems is to abandon the gross mind, which is the repository of all problems. If you live in the subtle mind, problems will no longer be solved through confrontation, but through an innate sense of grace and intuition. And, because problems will no longer be perceived as "personal," their existence will no longer be accompanied by a sense of unhappiness.

Q: *Is it possible to be always happy? What is your experience?*

BWS: [Laughing] Do you want the short answer or the long one?

Q: *The complete one.*

BWS: "Complete" is a good way of putting it. Since the age of eight, I've never been unhappy. I've been saddened by suffering, hatred, and events such as war, but it has never caused unhappiness. The subtle mind does not experience unhappiness as it is commonly understood; it feels these emotions, but in a very subtle sense. It has the profound ability to empathize and will respond appropriately in the moment to sorrowful circumstances.

I've wept at the sight of beauty or at the sight of an innocent infant. However, at a deeper level, the subtle mind is even above this response.

Q: *In your investigation have you found or discovered any "purpose" to life?*

BWS: The purpose of life is to ask the question, "What is the purpose of life?" Now that you're asking it, you have come to this purpose, which, by the way, is the sole reason for your birth.

Q: *But I've asked that question innumerable times and never received a satisfactory answer.*

BWS: And you never will if you continue to rely on a conceptual answer. The problem here is that you are asking a five-dollar transistor radio to listen to the sounds of the cosmos. Perhaps your real question is, "What is the meaning of *my* life?"

Q: *Essentially, yes.*

BWS: Since there is really no separate "you," there can never be a satisfactory answer concerning a subject that has no real existence. This is why you have never found one! It is like asking, "What happened to my car?" when in fact you never owned a car. No matter how many times you asked, you would never find a satisfactory answer!

Apart from the many ideas and concepts that make up "my life," where else would you find this separate sense of "I"? Please don't point to your body, since that body never uttered the word "I." Rather, you claimed the body as your own. If, in this very moment, you could ask the body, "Are you who I really am?" I'm sure—if it could respond at all—it would laugh or say, "I don't know what you're talking about." Most likely it would remain silent.

Well, if your body is not who you are, is it the endless chatter in your head? At least *it* seems to communicate. If you were to ask the voice where it's located, so that you could drop in for a visit and determine if you're biologically related to it, that would be great. However, as soon as you start addressing the voice it stops chattering. So it is nothing but a recorder-like mechanism running in your brain. Search as much as you like, you will never find it through the mind.

So we return to the question of meaning and purpose. Now that we know it's impossible to get a true answer from the limited, audiotape-like gross mind, I suggest that you look at this from another perspective—the point of view that allows you to observe this mental phenomenon from "spaciousness." The spaciousness that I'm referring to is the subtle mind, which is available at this very moment.

The subtle mind has always been available to all of humanity, yet it only rarely manifests because the foreground noise, based on thought, has dominated the mental structure. Just as the silence of the desert always exists, even when a radio is played in its midst, the subtle mind always exists in the background, regardless of the "noise" of thought. Throughout the centuries people have gained insight into the nature of this phenomenon and have come upon ways to silence thought and access the subtle mind.

THE DILEMMA OF CONDITIONING

Q: *I am an Attorney and I earn a good deal of money. I have a wonderful wife, three great kids, a nice home, etc. I am in the prime of my life and have everything I want, yet deep down I have an uncomfortable feeling that something is missing. I've struggled with this but don't know how to resolve it. This feeling troubles me a lot.*

BWS: In what way does this troubled feeling affect your life, either at home or at your job?

Q: *I've lost enthusiasm for my work and family. This scares me; sometimes I don't know who I am anymore.*

BWS: But you said earlier, with certainty, that you're a lawyer, a husband, and a father. Now you say that you don't know who you are. Maybe you're not looking at the whole picture. As a lawyer, you know how important it is to have *all* of the facts in a case so that a complete representation is available before proceeding. Am I correct?

Q: *That's exactly correct.*

BWS: Okay, so now you say that you feel something is "missing." Did you exclude something when you described who and what you were?

Q: *Like what?*

BWS: Like something even more fundamental about you than the things you listed.

Q: *Do you mean like being a Christian?*

BWS: No, you *became* a Christian. The other aspect I am referring to is something that was present when you were born.

Q: *My body?*

BWS: The body of a what?

Q: *An Irish-American lawyer? [He laughs at his answer.]*

BWS: Keep looking.

Q: *Oh! Do you mean me?*

BWS: Yes, yourself. When you listed the things that you were, you forgot to list your own innate sense of Being, which is more basic to your identity than those others, which are only concepts that overlay what you already are. It is quite humorous to see that you had difficulty remembering that you *are!* This is because you're a living concept-identity who has forgotten his true sense of self. Perhaps this is why you don't know who you are.

I'm sure you never forget that you're a lawyer when dealing with clients, or a husband when making love to your wife. Without the basic sense of Being, which functions as a foundation upon which these other identities sit, these concepts sooner or later come apart. When this happens, we come down with a case of "identity crisis."

Q: *So what shall I do to become fully human?*

BWS: Have you thought of what a human being is, independent of concepts?

Q: *I haven't really thought about it.*

BWS: [Pointing out a window toward a passing car] Do you see that object?

Q: *Do you mean that car?*

BWS: Yes. What is more basic to that object's nature, the *word* "car" or *the thing itself?*

Q: *I would say "the thing itself."*

BWS: Well, suppose "the thing itself" vanished? Let's put it another way: If all of the cars in the world vanished, what would happen to the word "car"? Take a moment to think about this as though you were in court and the judge asked you this same question. Think about it quite deeply.

Q: *I guess the word "car" would have no further use, so it would most likely vanish or simply float around uselessly in a kind of mental space.*

BWS: That's right. Now let's say, for example, that you were *the thing itself* on which the names "attorney, husband, father," etc., had been attached. And suppose you began to slowly lose a sense of who you really were, and to be strictly identified only with those names. Furthermore, since almost everyone in society agreed that this is what you are—since they were doing the same thing—this word became a kind of reality.

Additionally, since articles in periodicals and programs on TV joined in on this case of misidentification, additional consequences of these wrongly held beliefs began to grow, and become rampant— even among young children—until people lost the innate sense of their true self. This is exactly what is going on today. People are confused and suffering because they have surrendered their souls and become living concepts.

Q: *That is exactly what's happening. I see it with my kids.*

BWS: When we forget our true Being and become living concepts, we crave for more and more material goods in an addictive manner— all in an effort to satisfy the primal urge for satisfaction and contentment. All of the energy that's being expended on transient matters simply reinforces the belief that the gross mind is the sole reality.

Love is a basic need of humanity . . . it's what makes us human. But when the soul vanishes under the weight of appended concepts, like the word "car," it also tends to vanish or float uselessly like a phantom in some sort of mental space. The good news is that the subtle mind is always present, no matter how far we become lost in concepts and beliefs.

Q: *This sounds familiar. You seem to be describing my life.*

BWS: This situation is not unique to you. It describes the lives of most people. Your feeling of meaninglessness arises because you ignored your soul for a collection of loveless concepts, which burned themselves out at a critical moment in your life. And this feeling that something is missing is very accurate. What's missing is the original sense of yourself, your true being or presence.

Q: *Is there any way out of this dilemma?*

BWS: There is, but only on the condition that you seriously want to end it—at least as seriously as you would want to win an important court case, and with as much energy and fervor as you would put into that.

Q: *How is this done?*

BWS: First, without justifying any of your behavior, realize where the choices you've made in your life have led you. Second, if you choose to move ahead you will have to "walk away" from the gross mind, which is the seat and storehouse of the concepts that have caused this predicament.

Q: *How will this affect my life?*

BWS: It may reveal a quality of humanity within you that you feared may have been lost. Concurrent with the subsiding of the gross mind comes the arising of the subtle mind, whose very nature is love and freedom. You run the risk of experiencing true inner transformation.

THE ENDING OF THOUGHT

Q: *I recently read the following paragraphs that you wrote in an article:*

"Attention is an essential key to unlocking the human mind from its self-made prison. It is being held within these prison walls by the dual nature of thought that creates our limited sense of self and the world we see.

"Used properly, attention can overcome thought's rigid, dual conditioning, thereby freeing one from the myriad problems gross-mind thinking has created for all of humanity. By properly and consistently applying this attention energy, a person may become free from this conditioning."

How does attention accomplish this end?

BWS: Attention (focused awareness) is an instrument of the divine, and comes from the same divine source that formed the universe. Since it created material substance in the first place, it can uncreate it as well—similar to the way that one "uncreates" John Wayne's face when erasing a videotape. Attention also has the power to modify the mind's conditioning, transforming it from a gross, dual structure to a very subtle nondual structure.

Thought serves an entirely useful function once its destructive tendencies are removed. By "destructive," I mean its rigid, dual-oriented view, which is the source of all human conflict. This highly conditioned, egocentric movement splits and fragments life, which in reality is whole. Other than this little "flaw," there's nothing wrong with thought. Once it is freed of duality, thought will be desirable, especially if we want to enjoy a good game of bridge. When the gross nature of thought ends, a more subtle way of thinking will emerge— one that functions in a harmonious and judicious manner, is based in pure intelligence, and operates in the *totality* of life.

Q: *Your statement is rather far-reaching and general, wouldn't you say?*

BWS: Nevertheless, what I said is also accurate and readily experiencable. You mentioned the word "general," but in this application of attention it is really very specific. Water freezes at thirty-two degrees Fahrenheit. Yet, in actuality, each *particular* ice cube simultaneously freezes at that temperature as well. So, while the general is true, so is the particular. The greater and the lesser are not different from one another, even though the ego would deny such a view. It's something like a particular wave in the ocean deciding that it's an "individual wave" and that it wants to function independently in order to "do its own thing." What the wave doesn't realize is that, although it identifies itself with its temporary wave "form," in substance it is water. The wave hasn't been taught, and so doesn't realize that if its selfish individualistic actions could actually be carried out, it might endanger a large body of marine life.

In the same way, at the center of the problematic gross mind lies a self-centered ego that has grown large and greedy, feeding on its status in society as a false model for the good.

Q: *Isn't a certain amount of ego necessary for us to make progress?*

BWS: Yes, but from a limited viewpoint. Ultimately, both the gross mind and its ego creation will fade away. From the transcendental view, the consequences of self-motivated action threaten the extinction not only of the human race but of all forms of life. Existence has ways of handling ego-oriented aberrations. The subtle mind always has been and always will be the state-of-the-art human mind, because it contains within it a very *subtle* ego-sense that is highly efficient, intelligent, and oriented toward benefiting the whole.

Q: *Don't you feel that development of the ego contributes to the good of society?*

BWS: The current world situation reflects narcissistic thought that is glamorized in the media solely for profit. This profit motive has encouraged the media and entertainment producers to further promote the cult of individuality to a rapidly growing audience. This "philosophy of individuality" separates parts from the whole in the same way that a single finger on the hand might be primarily concerned with its own movement, and might eventually refuse to accept the essential needs of the entire hand and body. By continuing in this manner, the hand would soon malfunction and the body would lose an essential tool for survival.

The championing of the "rugged individualist" and of those athletes who are "tough competitors" is commonplace today. Such behaviors are now applauded as highly moral and held up to schoolchildren as a model they should follow. This attitude may breed generations of individual "selfish warriors" in all walks of life, including business and science and finally filtering down to individual family members. This loveless attitude has an alienating effect. It engenders rivalry, conflict, and violence; indeed, it threatens the whole. So, to answer the question: overdeveloped narcissistic thinking threatens everyone and requires a radical solution.

Q: *Are you saying that we should "stop thinking" in order to solve this dilemma?*

BWS: No. The ending of thought is not an option or possibility for most people, and it would surely mean the ending of social life as we know it. The solution is in the *modification* of thought, which would allow it to continue to function primarily as a tool, but to cease to be threatening to others.

Q: *This modification is not a form of thought control, is it?*

BWS: Not at all. It's something like placing a light-starved plant in the sunlight. In this example, the light is our own energy of attention. Because attention is beyond thought, its energy can hasten a natural, evolutionary modification of thought. This type of evolutionary change takes place continuously. For example, viruses are continually modifying themselves in order to avoid extinction from the drugs designed to eradicate them. This modification is proof of a latent intelligence within life. Life wants to survive! Thought, as it presently functions, has become more of a liability than an asset. It's time to trade in the old car that has become dangerous. Watch the evening news to verify this.

Current patterns of thinking, which are based in the gross mind, can take us to the moon but can't stop war. The thought-ridden gross mind will become violent if it senses that its material needs are threatened. Yet, at its source, the gross mind contains love and intelligence. We have seen the emergence of selfless love and pure intelligence in great teachers such as Jesus and Buddha, who fully embodied these qualities. When Jesus said "Love your neighbor as you love yourself," he was describing the natural quality of the subtle mind.

THE UNOBSTRUCTED VIEW

Q: *How does the notion of "wholeness" enter into what you're speaking of?*

BWS: Thought currently operates in a survival mode, which

promotes the individual at the expense of the whole of life, for which it seems to have little or no empathy. When dealing with the general problems of humanity, we're really only dealing with how those problems manifest and affect the lives of individuals.

Life is a balance, and that's what we're addressing here today. The movement of existence contains both the general and the specific forms of life within the unlimited whole. When viewed this way, the apparent "two" are intrinsically bound, and it is only thought—as it presently operates—that undermines our ability to discern this fact.

Q: *Twentieth-century psychology addresses some of these issues by "clarifying" thought. You use the word "attention." In substance, are insight and attention interchangeable?*

BWS: No. Although to the untrained ear they both sound like a "c-note," attention pulses at a higher harmonic. Psychological insight is the result of probing around in thought. Because thought is dualistic in nature, an ensuing insight will have within it the seed of an opposite and conflicting insight. Therefore, one can never arrive at certainty concerning any question. But the mind, in its quest for survival of the organism, needs certainty.

Psychologists work with an investigating instrument that is limited to definitions and concepts—movements that travel in a circular path, finally arriving back where they started. It's a zero sum game. This is why psychology, which is still based in thought, is incapable of solving "individual" problems. If this is the case, how could it possibly tackle the problems of humanity?

Q: *Are you saying that thought can never glimpse the whole of life, the gestalt of things?*

BWS: I'm saying just that! Thought only looks at life through the fragmented, kaleidoscopic instrument that it is. As far as thought is concerned, wholeness is a fantasy. However, just remove the kaleidoscope and look directly at the unobstructed view, and your soul will enter heaven right here on earth. This direct, unfragmented, unobstructed view is the "seeing" of your innate energy of attention.

Q: *How would you advise a person to proceed when using thought, so that they don't end up in a quagmire?*

BWS: Well, I'd say that it is dangerous to be looking at fragmentary ideas without looking simultaneously from a position of the unfragmented whole. The truth is that the movement of life is going on at many dimensions simultaneously. Try to envision the fact that, as we sit here talking, the earth is also spinning around the sun, our solar system is moving within the galaxy, the galaxy is moving within the universe, and so on.

See the truth of this awesome movement profoundly. Live with a sense of it in your consciousness every day. This is a clear and direct perception of attention; it is the true nature of the cosmic gestalt, which may flower within you and free your mind of its gross nature.

FROM THINKING TO PASSIVE LISTENING

Q: *You once suggested that if we ask thought a question, we should not accept any thought-based response, and that if we wait in silence, in a nonanswering state of mind, a nonverbal response will arise. Is this correct?*

BWS: Yes it's correct. I may want to add that the waiting is not an "expectant" waiting, but a passive waiting without *any* expectations of an arrival.

Q: *Are you saying that you don't think? Can thought actually go beyond itself?*

BWS: First of all, I *do* think. I like a good joke and find laughter very freeing. It opens space, especially in a group. It is my stimulant of choice, and there are no hangovers. When thought is asked a question that's beyond its capacity to answer—and if you realize that a verbal or thought-based response is not acceptable—thought will begin to chew on that very question. By your indicating that a thought-based answer will be vetoed, thought will immediately become quiet and shift into a silent and passive nonanswering state. This is the state of passive listening.

Q: *How does the mind react to all this once it is put into practice?*

BWS: The gross mind will actually be relieved that the decision to end its dominance has been made. Now, allow the spirit and energy of Being to carry you into the subtle mind. Existence will only heed your call when it feels a sincere and urgent need. When this need is deeply felt, the process of transformation has already begun.

Your true nature is beyond thought and beyond what you assumed were your limitations. Eight-year-old Bertram was in deep despair, and it was this despair that initiated his transformation.

Q: *What you're saying sounds very religious.*

BWS: It is religious, but it's also scientific. Albert Einstein said, "Science without religion is lame; religion without science is blind." One of the definitions of religion is "to bind again." These Attention Exercises are a way of returning to our source, which is divine.

LIVING IN THE "NOW" MEANS LIVING OUTSIDE OF THOUGHT

Q: *What is it that stops us, right now, from realizing the peace of our real nature?*

BWS: It is the cycle of compulsive thinking, which is dominated by a false sense of identity. This compulsive movement of thought is the nature of the gross mind. Attention (focused awareness) emanates from a higher source, beyond thought, and has the power, when energetically brought to bear on this compulsive movement, to bring it to an end. As a result, thought, and with it the entire mind, is transformed from a gross to a subtle quality.

Q: *I've read that it's important that we live "in the now." Is this an actual state of mind?*

BWS: Reference to "the now" can only be made in relation to ideas of past or future. Since neither of these ideas exists outside of thought, the concept of "now" is equally untrue.

Q: *Is there anything I can do, such as a change in lifestyle, etc., that will help accelerate my experience of the subtle mind?*

BWS: The subtle mind is always present, no matter what activity you're engaged in. Substituting activities or making changes in one's lifestyle is rarely necessary, though it is helpful to engage in activities that don't foster compulsive thinking or behavior.

THE EXPERIENCE OF UNLIMITED BEING

Q: *What's the difference between the Attention Exercises you recommend and traditional meditation?*

BWS: Traditional meditation is usually on an object. Because of this, the false subject (the "me") continues to function indefinitely. By using attention to step out of the role of subject, you immediately see that both subject and object (you and the world) depend on each other for their existence. When you're perceiving through the subtle mind, it becomes clear that subject and object are both concepts that result from dualistic thinking.

Q: *Do the Attention Exercises result in the annihilation of the ego? If this is the case, how can we continue to function in the world?*

BWS: What we take to be the ego is nothing more than a collection of thoughts anchored to the belief that each of us is a limited, separate individual. When we live in the subtle mind, the ego-sense becomes subservient and the experience of unlimited Being becomes dominant. This is *truly* living, and it's the only way to be in tune with who we really are. After all, why should we live such a limited life?

Q: *What is the experience of oneself and one's personality in the subtle mind?*

BWS: Let's start with the gross mind. Doesn't one experience what we think we are: a solid, distinctly named personality, separated by space from other distinctly named objects and people in the world? I know that "I am me" and I know that "I am not you."

Sometimes in meditation, when thought is quieted, we may experience ourselves as a separate and distinct "I am." In this case, the "me" in the "I am me" is less distinct. In the subtle mind the "I am" dissolves, and a barely experiencable, almost centerless "me-ness" arises. This me-ness is experienced as absolute silence and vast space. One may also feel a vibrating quality that resonates as "I am That."

THE HOLY GRAIL

Q: *Why do you say that the subtle mind and the Holy Grail are the same?*

BWS: To be more accurate, I said that the subtle mind *is* the Holy Grail.

Q: *Based on what evidence?*

BWS: The living experience of the subtle mind in which all nontruth has been purged.

Q: *How does that equate to the Holy Grail?*

BWS: The search for the Holy Grail is a search for absolute truth. The gross mind of humanity deals at best in relative truth, and therefore any searching within it for the Holy Grail (absolute truth) is in vain. It is only when the gross mind stops that the subtle mind emerges, and an *absence* of nontruth is exposed—not as an idea but as an actual experience. The Old Testament provides an insight into this state with the passage "Be still, and know that I am God." I would interpret it this way: "When you are truly still, you will know the 'you' to be God." Try it right now; turn your attention inward and silently ask yourself to "Be still!"

Q: [After a pause] *Is this silence the Holy Grail?*

BWS: It is the silence of God's love.

RESTORING FREEDOM

Q: *I'd like to read you something that you said in an interview:*

> "In a great cosmic drama being played out in the theatre of the mind, the ego—for its own pleasure—has trapped and subverted attention by splitting its power and holding it hostage as thought in the field of duality. Through the simple act of discovering where it is located, attention awakens and ends the drama by freeing itself. This done, the peace of Eden once more reigns upon the earth."

Were you only speaking metaphorically when you said this?

BWS: No.

Q: *How is this an accurate statement, and if so, how does it apply to the* *gross and subtle aspects of mind that you refer to?*

BWS: It obviously applies to both of these aspects of mind. To understand what I said, we must first recognize that awareness is an energy given to human beings to provide us with the ability to know ourselves and become free.

RESTORING THE ABILITY TO MEDITATE

Q: *I've been meditating for years to calm my mind, but I've made very little progress. I feel sure that living in the subtle mind is where I want to be. The problem is that I never find it easy to settle into a tranquil, meditative state. Thoughts are going on like mad, and I'm unable to stop them. I often become discouraged and have stopped meditating for long periods. How do I quiet my mind and overcome the resistance I've built up to meditation?*

BWS: When you learn to quiet your mind, the resistance to sitting in meditation will end naturally. What is your name?

Q: *Ken.*

BWS: Ken, here's a principle that is always helpful in handling these two problems: "When Ken *is*, meditation *is not*. " When I speak of meditation, I don't mean sitting quietly in a certain posture. For me, meditation means to have a mind that is *in a state* of meditation. According to what you've told me, you've never truly meditated, since a meditative mind is silent and empty.

Q: *The problem is, how do I get to that?*

BWS: Let's first establish that Ken *is* the gross mind, according to our little principle that says: "When Ken *is*, meditation *is not*." Or, to put it another way: "When the gross mind *is*, the subtle mind *is not*." The subtle mind *is itself* a state of meditation, and the gross mind *is not* a state of meditation. Is this clear? So how does one seem to get to the subtle mind? The paradox is, one doesn't *get* to the subtle mind at all; one only has to "banish" the gross mind in the same way one banishes images on a television screen: by not looking at them. It's a matter of looking somewhere else.

Q: *What should I look at?*

BWS: Something that's always right where you are—in front of you, behind you, above you.

Q: *Are you speaking of space?*

BWS: Exactly. When you look at space, you cannot be looking at the television pictures in your mind—your thoughts. No thoughts, no gross mind. The absence of the gross mind leaves what? This bring us back to our earlier principle: When the gross mind is not . . .

Q: *While you were speaking, I was carefully studying the space in the room and suddenly the gross mind shut off. Is this the silence of the subtle mind?*

BWS: Yes. What you did is called "Locating" and is an important part of the Attention Exercises. After doing this for a while, you'll rarely go back to watching mind television.

Rehabilitation of the Spirit

Q: *When you speak of the subtle mind, it feels familiar, as though I've been there before. Once I began to cry just out of relief, knowing that there is truly a place where I can have peace. But then I start to think that perhaps what I believe is just an idea, and the happy feeling vanishes. This happens quite a bit. Is there anything I can do to find out the truth about this?*

BWS: Yes, there is. First, understand the limits of thought, which is only useful for engaging the world in a mechanical and limited way. For instance, thought relies on information derived from other people's thoughts or ideas in order to arrive at the best way to build a bridge or bake a pie. However, if you ask thought what love is, the best it can do is recite a love poem or tell you about the chemical response of the body of a person in love. This is not the answer we're looking for, since the experience of being in love is about as close as we can ever get to knowing the truth about what love *actually* is. Not only is it useless, but it can even be risky for you to accept ideas and concepts about spiritual matters without first experiencing them yourself.

You are a divine being. Any answer that you seek must come from your own deep spiritual introspection. In other words, turn your attention inward and wait for grace. If you're patient, I assure you that the answer concerning that place of inner peace will arrive by itself. I've seen this happen many times. The subtle mind of peace is yours for the asking; you only need to turn down the volume of the noisy gross mind.

Q: *Turning down the mind is not always easy—especially when problems arise. It seems to be the only place to go for answers.*

BWS: Affairs of the heart and the spirit are matters of feeling or intuition. You're better off asking your pocket calculator about the meaning of life than asking thought; at least the calculator won't mislead you. The material world is thought's arena. Serious questions concerning the inner life are beyond the limited capacity of thought, which is restricted to ideas and opinions. Thought can recite poems about what life is, or offer scientific descriptions of what life may be, but in the end it will fail to arrive at the heart of the matter. Whatever you may "think" will never be Truth; at best it will be theory or speculation. In matters of the Spirit, trust your heart rather than the opinions of others, including mine.

AWAKENING FROM THE DREAM

Q: *You have said that the so-called "individual life" is merely a dream that's played out in the theatre of the gross mind, and that when one awakens from this dream, one may then truly understand the implications of the word "God." I don't know—my life is very real to me. My problems are also very real, and they require very real solutions. How can you say that it's just a dream?*

BWS: First, let's start with what we all accept as a dream and work from there. While asleep, we are somehow magically transported into a different reality than the daytime reality we're familiar with. There, we may encounter people who have died years before and greet them as if they were still alive. In this dream-drama, we carry on conversations, and it all appears to be very real. You may suddenly find yourself in a jungle, being pursued by a ferocious tiger that you believe is getting closer and closer. Your heart is pounding with terror. Now, let's just imagine that I suddenly appear in your dream, and from behind a bush shout, "Wake up—you're only dreaming!" What would you say in the dream?

Q: *In the dream, I'd probably say "Get out of my way!" and would likely throw you to the ground and continue to run.*

BWS: Why wouldn't you listen to me when I strongly indicated to you that this was only a dream?

Q: *Because the dream appeared to be real.*

BWS: So how would you escape from the dream tiger? Would you pray that a dream policeman with a dream gun would arrive and rescue you? How would you get out of this frightening dilemma?

Q: *I'm not sure.*

BWS: What is the one absolutely certain way to save yourself from the jaws of the tiger?

Q: *An absolutely certain way?*

BWS: Yes, guaranteed!

Q: *Do you mean to wake up?*

BWS: Indeed. By your waking up, the tiger will vanish and there's no longer any jungle to be found. You discover that you never left your bed. The only truth in the dream were the words spoken by the person in your nightmare who said "Wake up—you're only dreaming!" Yet you refused to accept this truth then and refuse to accept it now, hoping that some dream character in this waking dream might rescue you from your problems.

Q: *But this life-dream seems so real!*

BWS: When you sleep, don't the events in the dream seem to be equally real?

Q: *Yes, they do.*

BWS: Whether you're dreaming while awake or asleep, only awakening will banish your fears in the same way it banished the tiger.

SUBTLE MIND/BUDDHA MIND

Q: *In the following verse, the* Maitri Upanishad *(3.4) states:*

"Samsara [the world] is no more than one's thought.
With effort one should therefore cleanse the thought.
What one thinketh, that one becomes,
This is the eternal mystery."

Does this verse mean, for example, that if your attention goes to a disturbing image you actually experience the emotional disturbance at that moment?
BWS: Even simpler. I would interpret it this way: When you put your attention on anxiety-provoking thoughts, you will *become* an anxious person. This is because you identify with the content of the gross mind. In other words, in the gross mind, you *are* what you think.
Q: *In what way?*
BWS: Where were you born and where do you reside?
Q: *I was born in, and currently live in, Great Britain.*
BWS: So you're British?
Q: *Yes, I think of myself that way.*
BWS: That's exactly what the Upanishad is saying. You have *become* the reality of your thoughts. What if your mind didn't contain images of being British—let's say all of your ideas about being British were accidentally deleted, as in a computer—would you still feel British?
Q: *No, I guess not.*
BWS: Once, while creating a new Attention Exercise, I inadvertently stumbled upon a clue as to what might have happened to the Buddha as he sat under the Bodhi Tree. A few hours before this revelation, a former student came to visit me. At the time, a friend was also present. The visitor spent quite a bit of time relating a poignant tale of woe. About one hour after the former student left, my friend remarked that the visitor's story continued to disturb him. I thought this would be a good opportunity to test the new exercise, which was meant to dispel the arising of disturbing thoughts. I had long been convinced that attention, which perceives the content of mental images, *creates and experiences as real* what it perceives.

My friend's attention was on the images of the distressing story he had recently heard and found to be upsetting. I asked him to relocate his attention away from the world of disturbing mental images, to the objective world right in front of him and vigorously keep his attention there. Less than a minute later, he smiled and reported that the troublesome images had disappeared, and that his mind had become empty.

I was intrigued by my friend's remark because it reminded me of the Buddha's moment of enlightenment. Just prior to his enlightenment, the Buddha's mind was filled with undesirable thoughts and in a state of agitation. Determined to dispel the bothersome mental images, he vowed to continue until full enlightenment dawned. Using the power of attention, he located his awareness *away* from the image-ridden mind and entered a blissful state of emptiness.

What prompted both of these mind-emptying occurrences was the shift of attention from the world of mental images to the peaceful space of the subtle mind. This is the basic principle of the "Locating" procedure, which I had just completed as the primary Attention Exercise. When you keep your attention in the space of the objective world, it cannot go back to the world of mental images, since it cannot be in both places at the same time.

Q: *But most people who practice meditation have not awakened, at least not in the way Buddha did.*

BWS: I truly believe that we all have the Buddha-nature within us and are certainly destined to awaken. Some of us are just early risers.

NATURAL LOVE

Q: *What about the kind of selfless love of which Jesus spoke? How does this connect with the notion of the subtle mind?*

BWS: It connects in a very direct way. Wholeness is basic to the quality of the subtle mind. Treating others as you would have them treat you is a reality rather than an aphorism. The first and last step in human transformation would be from the naturally competitive sense of the gross mind to the naturally cooperative sense of the subtle mind; from the prevailing state of "mine is mine" to an enlightened state of "mine is thine." In other words, the transformed state makes it entirely natural for people to cooperate with one another, since this sense of natural cooperation has its basis in unity and love.

Change Is Now or Never

Q: *I feel that I need more freedom in my life, but I'm not sure what to do about it or what actually makes me feel bound.*

BWS: First find out what the nature of the prison is and how you got there.

Q: *I believe it has to do with my fear of change.*

BWS: In what way would you change if you were not afraid?

Q: *I'd make my life simpler by getting rid of a lot of unnecessary baggage that keeps me financially trapped in a meaningless job.*

BWS: Well, what's stopping you?

Q: *Fear of unknown consequences.*

BWS: That fear is your self-imposed prison.

Q: *But the fear may be a good thing. It may be a warning not to do something impractical without thinking about it more carefully.*

BWS: How long have you been thinking it over?

Q: *For several years.*

BWS: Have you come to any practical conclusions in those years?

Q: *Yes. I see that I must do something to change my life, and, at the same time, I'm too frightened to make a move that would accomplish this. My conclusion is that I'm stuck! And I need to figure out a way to get unstuck.*

BWS: So in the meantime you remain imprisoned by fear of the unknown?

Q: *That's an accurate way of putting it.*

BWS: So you prefer to remain in prison?

Q: *Someday I'll figure how to get out.*

BWS: But this present moment is the only moment that will ever exist. "Someday" is a projection of your mind, and as such will never arrive. Today is the "someday" you spoke of yesterday. So, to truly change, one must change right *now*!

THE SILENT SPACE OF GOD'S LOVE

Q: *You stress that it's imperative that one "Locate" and "Be Still" prior to doing any of the Attention Exercises. What's the reason for this?*

BWS: We normally use thought to operate in the physical world. This is simply a function of the gross mind, which measures problems and finds solutions through book knowledge, ideas, and concepts. This technical capacity can never work when we're attempting to measure our inner nature, which is immeasurable.

It is imperative that we "Locate" and "Be Still" prior to doing an Attention Exercise in order to bypass the limited instrument of thought. This allows us to see *directly* through the power of attention.

Q: *How is this accomplished?*

BWS: By "Locating," attention is brought away from thoughts and images and into the actual physical space of the world. Next, thought is told to "Be Still." When attention is kept on that inner stillness for a period of time, the subtle silence may become the quality of one's everyday mind. This is what is called living in the subtle mind.

Q: *What is the nature of this subtle silence?*

BWS: If I had to put it into words, I would say it was "the silent space of God's love."

THE EVOLUTION OF THE GROSS MIND

Q: *Does the subtle mind have a fixed psychological center?*

BWS: Although it doesn't contain an image of itself as an individual personality, the subtle mind can recall images of the past when necessary. These images are devoid of ownership by an individual ego, since the robust psychological center that existed prior to transformation is no longer there.

In the gross mind, an image of a past event might be quite traumatic. In the subtle mind, this same image would have no more psychological impact than a fleeting cloud. When the mind becomes subtle, the self-centered ego-sense does not arise.

Q: *Is this a permanent state?*

BWS: It is permanently available to those who wish to live in it. It is more natural and lasting than thought, in the same manner that the space around us is more lasting than the objects contained within it. Notice how this space is silent and boundless yet contains everything. In the same way, the subtle mind contains the space, intelligence, and love of the living cosmos. It is the *active* aspect of the unmanifest, eternal Source.

Q: *Is this why you refer to the subtle mind as the intelligence of the living universe?*

BWS: Let me explain this by referring to the *Tao Te Ching*. According to Lao-Tzu, the Tao is the eternal Source from which life manifested. The subtle mind is an aspect of this eternal Source. And, although it contains within it each of the "ten thousand myriad things" (including the human race), its eternal and unmanifest nature is clearly perceived. However, when the mind is active in its gross aspect, this same manifestation is seen to *appear* separate from its Source. This is due to the movement of thoughts and images that make up the gross mind and is responsible for the feeling of being a "separate" individual.

Q: *From the point of evolution, was it necessary for the gross mind to emerge?*

BWS: Yes, it was. The evolutionary process required a symbol-oriented instrument for the development of language and the measurement and manipulation of physical matter—all for the purpose of aiding physical survival. The gross mind functions well when utilized strictly for technical purposes. For example, it operates as an organizing structure that scientists use in the exploration of the material universe.

The problem for humanity arose when this measuring instrument—which is dualistic by nature—turned inward and attempted to measure the immeasurable soul, according to its own limited nature. Caught in the duality of "right" and "wrong," it divided humanity and "fell asleep" into a dream of individuation, where people felt separate from others and consequently competed for their own "personal" survival. The "dreamer" had completely forgotten that his or her eternal Source was One. The way to reawaken to this truth is through the subtle mind, which is *whole* and always intimately connected to the eternal, unmanifest Source.

Q: *Are you implying that there are two minds?*

BWS: Not at all. The subtle and gross minds are only aspects of the unmanifest Source, which is who we are in truth. The subtle mind is that aspect of mind that is in natural harmony with the physical universe. The gross, egocentric mind governs the life of the apparent "individual." Transformation occurs when the gross mind experientially encounters the intelligence and harmony of the eternal Source and is rendered subtle. Remember, these are just *aspects* of the one unmanifest Source from which they emerged.

Q: *How would living in the subtle mind affect life on an everyday basis?*

BWS: Because the subtle mind is nonlinear by nature, it can experience the infinite intelligence of the Source. As a result, the subtle mind is then able to express the wholeness of life in its interaction with all of existence. A society grounded in wholeness would be a return to an enlightened Eden and would endow humanity with true wisdom—the original intended goal of religion.

THE FLOWERING OF CONSCIOUSNESS

Q: *I would like to ask you a very basic question that my seven-year-old daughter asked me, and I was unsure how to answer her. The question is, "Why was I born?"*

BWS: Asking this question is a necessary trigger that helps provoke a search for its answer. The question of life's meaning lies like a dormant seed within the psyche of every human being, planted there by consciousness as a way to rediscover its existence *as* consciousness. The seed may remain quiet until some life event stirs it and it begins to flower. The first sign of this flowering is the asking of the question itself.

For some, this flowering occurs in childhood; for others, the question may only arise at the time of death. But the question *will* be asked! It is part of our purpose and destiny to ultimately discover who we are and why we were born. If you agree with what has been said, try to explain this to your child in a very simple way. Since she spontaneously asked the question, I'm certain she is ready to understand your answer.

Q: *How can I encourage her to continue this search for truth?*

BWS: By the example you set in your own search for meaning in everyday life. Since she asked the essential question on her own, she will tend to absorb occurrences that may lead to its answer. She now has no choice in the matter. The flowering has begun; just don't put obstacles in its way, and nourish it with the light of love.

THE DISCOVERY OF YOURSELF IS THE GOAL

Q: *I'm forty-five years old, and I find that my life is primarily tedious, boring, and without meaning. I'm searching for something that will excite and thrill me—not outwardly but inwardly. I'm looking for something that will raise my spirits. I've been involved with music for many years, and find that what previously excited me no longer does, and is in fact quite limited. Also, I've recently taken up the practice of meditation. What can you do for me? [Laughs] I mean, what can you suggest?*

BWS: I'm glad you added the word "inwardly." Otherwise, with words like "excite" and "thrill" I might have suggested the local tavern. But if it's *inward* excitement and thrills you want, I have a very workable plan to extricate you from your chronic doldrums. Would you like to take a new direction that would include within it a sense of deep peace, beauty, and love?

Q: *Yes, I'd love all of that!*

BWS: The discovery of yourself is the goal of this plan. The method is to turn inward to your true home and awaken to your real—and, to use your word—"thrilling" self. You see, you have never left this abode where you dream the sorrowful dream you believe to be your life. Would awakening from this dream fit your present needs?

Q: *It would indeed! When do we start?*

BWS: Right now. First of all, really slow down. Now, take a very deep breath, turn your attention inward, and just be very still.

TRUE ART POINTS TO THE UNLIMITED

Q: *I am an artist, and I find that in the field of art there is the artist and a final product that he or she created. In meditation, however, there is no tangible product that a meditator can produce. Yet, despite this difference, there seems to be a similar "harmonic" between art and meditation.*

BWS: The uniting element in both is the search for Truth. Art seeks the ideal in *form*, while meditation seeks the ideal in *spirit*. The artist's ideal remains material, but the meditator's ideal transcends the material to go into the realm of the spiritual. They both seek the beauty of Truth, each in their own dimension.

This search for perfection has within its movement a fragrance of the divine. One immediately senses this fragrance in profound art and profound meditation. I'm not surprised that you've taken up meditation, since it helps one to transcend the need for material perfection in favor of pure immaterial perfection. This may be what you were initially seeking when you first became drawn to art. Ultimately, the soul will reject anything less than the purity of being established in the Eternal.

Q: *Are you suggesting that I give up art?*

BWS: Not at all. Art, which creates a form of limited beauty, has its place in life. It acts as a pointer toward the beauty of the Unlimited. But if you wish to discover ultimate Truth, meditation is the formless vehicle that will take you there.

Q: *Is the energy of attention also a vehicle?*

BWS: It is the ideal vehicle. Attention is an express train that carries one directly into awakening.

Love Is What You Are

Q: *I am often so enmeshed in problems that I feel as if I'm being smothered. I'm a widow with two children and live in a middle-class suburban community. I don't live excessively—either socially or financially—yet the burden of day-to-day living has become overwhelming. I can't seem to find any personal space, which I feel is very necessary. I hardly sleep and feel a growing sense of nonspecific anxiety. Is there a realistic solution to this?*

BWS: You say you wish for a "realistic" solution, but what would you consider to be an "unrealistic" solution?

Q: *Deserting my family and retiring to the South Seas would be unrealistic. I guess what I'm asking for is a* practical *solution.*

BWS: I would say that you're at least halfway to finding it.

Q: *I'm not sure what you mean by that.*

BWS: To know that you have a problem, to be candid about it and courageous enough to articulate its nature to another person as clearly as you did is an enormous first step in finding a solution. Because you have had an insight into the cause of your ailment, a practical method of treatment can be applied.

Q: *What would that require?*

BWS: You have described a situation in which you become

overwhelmed by the mechanics of life, but I have not heard a word about love.

Q: *I love my children very much.*

BWS: Do you love your entire life as well?

Q: *That question has never entered my mind.*

BWS: When you become as overwhelmed by love for your *entire* life as you have been by your problems, the solution you seek will find you.

Q: *Where does one find that love?*

BWS: It is within you this very moment. You merely have to turn your attention inward and face it. *Love is what you are.* See this and peace of mind will reign. Awakening to ever-present love, which is what you really are, is the only solution.

THE NATURAL COMPASSION OF AWAKENING

Q: *I recently read that, for true spiritual awakening to take place, the ego must be gotten rid of. Is this even possible? And, if so, what would be the nature of my existence in such a situation?*

BWS: Upon awakening you exist *inwardly* in a state of egoless existence, yet outwardly as a person with an "apparent" personality similar to the one that presently exists. The difference is that you no longer *identify* with the personality but continue to use it in everyday social activities.

This is something similar to what actors do: they appear to be the personality of the character they portray, always knowing that this is just an appearance and not who they are in truth.

People who see an awakened one generally mistake their outward personality to be their primary sense of identity, and often have trouble seeing otherwise. Living in a state of enlightenment, one lives "in the world, but not of it."

Q: *What, then, keeps the realized person from just "walking away" from the world?*

BWS: Along with the realization that we're really not separate from anyone else comes a profound sense of love for all. One sees the suffering of the world in the same way that one would see a child screaming in the midst of a frightening nightmare. Rather than "walk away," one comforts the child and awakens him from the terror in order for him to see that he was only dreaming.

There is a natural compassion and sense of responsibility that flowers with awakening.

OBSERVE WITH YOUR EYES AND NOT WITH YOUR MIND

Q: *Bertram, when I look at the world today I see chaos, war, genocide, and the amassing of wealth by a very few, which results in the suffering of millions of people, including innocent children. Are you not emotionally moved by these conditions? Also, do you see a way out of this nightmare?*

BWS: Yes, I am very moved by the suffering of humanity. Regarding your second question, the answer is also yes, and let me tell you why. There is a hummingbird feeder outside our dining room window, and I often study the birds as they feed. I'm constantly impressed at the intelligent design of a hummingbird's body as a survival apparatus. It can hover over a feeder or a flower and has a needle-like beak that fits perfectly into the blossom while its unique tongue unrolls to gather in the nectar. This is awesome! The implication of this is astounding, and it provides a clue as to why I feel life can transcend its nightmarish condition in any given moment.

The same divine love and intelligence that went into assuring the survival of the hummingbird transformed an eight-year-old downhearted boy. As a personal witness to the power of divine love, I can assure you that the same love will bring about a transformation of the human mind and heart.

Q: *Can you give me a scientific basis for your optimism?*

BWS: I really can't argue at the level of science. I can speak only from personal experience, which is not arguable, because what I see is not measurable by science or any other discipline. But if anyone is interested in experiencing even the smallest fragrance of the miracle of which I speak, sit silently and study a hummingbird as it feeds, without trying to understand or analyze.

Observe with your eyes and not your mind. If you're very still and sensitive to the moment, you may see a miracle; you may be witness to the power of divine love in action that is beyond the limits of science.

God Is Revealed in the Still Mind

Q: *I have been a churchgoer since I was a child. I devoutly believe in God and pray several times a day. Recently, I've been feeling that my prayers have lost some of their power and I don't know why. My question is: Do you believe in the power of prayer?*

BWS: Yes, I do.

Q: *How can I regain some of the former power when addressing the Almighty?*

BWS: Let me answer by asking you a question. When you pray, where do you address your prayers?

Q: *To God in heaven.*

BWS: Do you believe that God is omnipresent and exists everywhere?

Q: *Yes, I do believe that God exists everywhere.*

BWS: In that case, God must also exist within you. Is that right?

Q: *Well, if you put it that way, it's not possible for God not to be within me.*

BWS: Both within you and right in this very moment?

Q: *Yes, right in this moment.*

BWS: Perhaps if you would directly access God, who is within you and closer than your breath, you might regain the power of prayer that you seek.

Q: *I see what you mean but I'm not sure how to get there.*

BWS: Let's take our lead from Psalm 46:10 in the Old Testament, which states, "Be still, and know that I am God." It is in this "stillness"—which is the quiet of the subtle mind—that God is revealed. Would you be willing to take a few minutes to look within and be still right now?

Q: *Yes, I would like that.*

BWS: Okay.

Q: [After a period of silence] *I think I've tasted the real power of prayer for the first time.*

TALKS WITH STUDENTS

PART THREE

"I entered into unknowing,
and there I remained unknowing
transcending all knowledge."
—ST. JOHN OF THE CROSS

Pointers on the Way

The word "intelligence" comes from the Latin *intellegre*, which means to realize the deeper meaning of something, to understand the whole of it. Because the gross mind is incapable of seeing the *totality* of life, it can only understand the present in reference to the past. Based in thought, which gives rise to time, the gross mind can never see the *truth* of a present event. For this reason, it is unable to change, and is, therefore, incapable of perceiving the deeper, divine intelligence that is required for transformation to take place.

The subtle mind, on the other hand, does not allow thoughts of the past to corrupt its ability to fully experience the present. It naturally grasps the larger meaning of the totality of existence, and responds to life circumstances accordingly. This ability of "whole-viewing" is essential if there is to be true spiritual transformation.

The following insights reveal the quality of *intellegre*—the divine love and wisdom that is the natural basis of the subtle mind.

PEACE OF MIND

When awareness energy (attention) is turned inward toward its source (and held there), the illusion of a separate "me" is removed and one faces the Eternal Self.

When this same awareness energy is turned outward, it "makes real" images of the world, and the illusory drama called "my life" comes into being.

If, throughout the day, we notice when attention drifts outwardly, and gently turn it back toward itself, deep inner peace will flower within.

INNER TRANSFORMATION

Inner transformation is the movement from the "I am me"-oriented consciousness, which is based on a self-centered individual, to the "I Am" consciousness, which is selfless, universally oriented consciousness.

Inner transformation is intrinsic to all human beings in the same way that flying is inherent in birds and hunting is inherent in lions. However, it is required that these natural abilities be taught, just as adult birds and lions teach their offspring how to fly and hunt.

All war, hate, fear, and anxiety—in short, all suffering of humankind—is due only to the ignorance of our divine nature. Inner transformation is nothing more than awakening to this divine nature, which is naturally inherent within us.

Only by turning our attention to our real nature will we be awakened to a greater reality. That which we already *are* is that which we seek. However, this must be put into practice and directly experienced.

The Breaking of Conditioning

When we see the illusory and insubstantial nature of all of existence, then the ending of time takes place, and with it the ending of all accumulated knowledge (the past).

To test this proposition, we need only imagine "deleting" all of our knowledge that currently exists in the form of words and concepts and see what occurs.

The Flowering of the Subtle Mind

When we actually "see" the limited nature of the gross mind, the authority that is bestowed upon it is negated, and its chaotic nature comes to an end. This is the transformation of human consciousness and the immediate flowering of the subtle mind.

This is the only *complete* transformation available. All other forms are limited, and make "adjustments" within the limits of the time-bound gross mind.

Consciousness Awakening to Consciousness

The moment a shift to the subtle mind occurs, we may look at others and see that we are only looking at ourselves; consciousness has awakened to itself and is gazing into its own eyes.

Awakening occurs spontaneously when one is *aware* of being aware.

Time exists only as a mental concept and not as a physical object or universal law. Awakening means to wake up from the illusion of time-bound consciousness into the timeless here-and-now of intuitive, knowing consciousness.

THOUGHT AND REALITY

Remaining with *any* idea of an experience kills the essence of that experience. It is like binding the flowering of life within time in order to capture a single moment of its beauty—which instantly kills the flower.

FREEDOM FROM ILLUSION

Give up all definitions you have created about yourself and the world. This will take you into the subtle mind and the freedom you have always sought!

Freedom is *now or never*! It is not something you can gain or lose, nor is it something to be achieved in the future. Freedom is what you *are* when the gross mind submits to the inherent freedom of the subtle mind.

If you want to be free, then remain inwardly *still*! This stillness opens the door to the bliss of eternal freedom.

The Way to Enlightenment

All ideas and concepts about yourself are false and are responsible for creating the illusion that keeps you from actually *being* who you really are, right now. Actually *seeing* this truth is the expression of enlightenment.

Enlightenment is knowing that, other than a few thousand years of other people's explanations about life, you know absolutely *nothing*!

You will be enlightened when you stop trying so hard to become enlightened. Take a deep breath, be still, and welcome the Eternal! Let go of any wish for or ideas of enlightenment. All this is part of the world of becoming, which is nothing more than the world of the time-based mind.

Awakening to Eternal Consciousness

When we perceive ourselves as a self-interested point around which the rest of the world revolves, and see that every other person experiences himself the same way, we gain an insight into how people have always experienced the world. Upon seeing this, we may experience the universal quality of consciousness that exists in us and in every other person.

Individual consciousness then rushes forward to join and intermingle intimately with the consciousness of all others. This enjoining of consciousness is the *sole* purpose of human life.

✳ The *surrendering* of the search for a purpose in life—other than one's existence as pure consciousness—is the primary and perhaps only step required for spiritual transformation.

To honestly say "I don't know" regarding the meaning of anything (including the meaning of this statement), and to feel the truth of this profoundly, is virtue itself and the innocence of the subtle mind.

THE MEANING OF LIFE

What is the meaning of Life? Whatever we say or think about it can *never* be it.

What you are *doing and being this very moment* contains the entire meaning of your life. Stay attentive to this moment, because "right now" *is the only life you will ever have*. The truth of this will not change in either ten minutes or ten years. Try to see if you can ever lose the "right now" that is your life.

Any answer about the meaning of life, other than the joy of what you're doing "right now," is only speculation or mental projection.

All the meaning of life lies in the *living of it*, and only you can do that. Therefore, only *you* can know its meaning. The first step in discovering this meaning is to stop asking others to explain it to you.

SPIRITUAL GOALS

If you want to be really wealthy, devote your life's energy to gaining spiritual assets. Obtaining material wealth without knowledge of your divine nature is true poverty.

Achieving peace of mind can never be a *personal* goal. The peace you seek is the ground of Being, which contains God's love for all manifestation. Peace can only be achieved when the "you" is transformed from personal to impersonal. Then, peace alone exists.

Drop all goals this very second except the goal of being exactly who you already are. If I said to you, "Have a goal to someday become a human being," you would think I was confused because you know that you *already are* a human being. When you ask me how to become a realized being, I think that you are confused, for what I see before me is the eternal soul.

TRANSFORMATION AND THE SUBTLE MIND

The transformation from the gross mind to the subtle mind provides a much greater context to our lives. Then, all of humanity becomes our family and we are no longer limited to a particular race, religion, or community.

This transformation brings with it an intuitive way of being that is untouched by the divided nature of thought. It is all-inclusive and reveals the only true "common ground" between all of existence.

Our environment influences our belief systems, and we live our life accordingly. It tells us "who we are," and we believe it as if this were the highest reality. This blind acceptance automatically places us in conflict with other people's belief systems, which ultimately leads to conflict and discord.

True transformation requires that the gross mind move beyond its conditioning and limitations to discover authentic common ground— the ground of our true nature. With this discovery comes the awareness of the fundamental commonality of all life. This is truly living in the subtle mind.

The subtle mind is an aspect of mind in which differences are seen but are subtle enough not to cause any sense of separation. A person might say, "I am Swedish. However, I am a human being first and I see all humanity as my family." The subtle mind has the ability to recognize this greater context in our life and in all of nature.

In this transformation, the boundaries of reality have expanded to such a degree that the "Perfume of the Divine" lingers and permeates every aspect of our daily life.

THE TRUTH OF ABSENCE

You can only know Truth in the absence of nontruth. Using words as a vehicle is an addiction that will never get you there.

We must enter into absence directly. In the absence of "I" we are instantly enveloped by the bliss of our real nature. Are you different from this absence?

Living in the world is not a hindrance to realizing Truth. The real obstacle is believing in the dream called "me." Awaken to the *absence* of this bogus self and discover your real home.

By entering the subtle mind, one is immediately plunged into timeless, silent space. The fixed psychological ego-center dies to this absence, along with all its images and concepts. Even the notion of a "now" is nonexistent. From this place one may orient to a subtle transient center for the sake of carrying on ordinary social activities.

SURRENDER

Surrender *right now* to all of existence, to the totality of life as you know it. Stop resisting until you become surrender itself. Peace is always available right where you are, through the power of surrender.

Peace of mind comes immediately upon the surrender of the domineering gross mind. Transformation results from the submission of the illusory individual to the truth of pure Being.

Undefine yourself and you undefine the world! Your freedom depends *only* upon the surrender of your ego-centered definitions. The experience of universal love will surely follow.

The intuitive subtle mind recognizes life afresh in each moment. It has surrendered the past and as such does not carry the burden of ancient prejudices, the source of all conflict and discord.

LIVING IN THE SPACE OF FREEDOM

You are the fixed center in which the totality of existence moves. Real freedom is to cease identifying with the false "me"—the well-developed and nurtured set of identity concepts that you are not.

BIRTH, DEATH, AND ETERNITY

Birth and death are myths—not options that you have. *Be still* right now and meet your eternal Self.

You were never born and you will never die. You just "showed up" and claimed a body. The eternal "you" is always *right here and now.*

You are the eternal spirit. There is never a time when you are nonexistent.

TRUTH AND NON-TRUTH

"I think, therefore I am" is correct only from the point of view of the gross mind. To the contrary, the subtle mind would just say, "I am."

Don't desire to know truth. Rather, see nontruth for what it is. By your seeing the limited nature of nontruth, the infinite truth will automatically embrace you, and bliss will be your natural disposition.

Unname yourself and you will awaken to "what is." Upon seeing the *implication* of this, you will instantly realize your infinite nature. The unnamed world will automatically reveal to you the truth of "what actually is."

Before being named, the world was what it is. After being named, it became what it was not. To see the truth of this, simply unname the world!

Harmony

When you *include* the seer in the seeing, harmony is everywhere; heaven is never anywhere else but *here*.

Harmony in the world depends solely on the degree of harmony within you.

To know everything, you must first be willing to give up all knowledge.

Our True Nature

Living in the subtle mind will enable you to discover your own perfection and the perfection of the entire world. It cannot be otherwise, because perfection is your very nature.

Wake up! Live in the subtle mind right now. The joy of your perfection will permeate the hearts of those around you. They cannot resist it because it is their nature also.

You arrived in this world wrapped in perfection. By turning your attention inward, you can recover that subtle flawlessness which you always are.

The worrisome ego is nothing more than a bogus "you." See the truth of this condition this very moment and your joyous nature will inundate every part of your life.

The Absolute and the Relative

The absolute contains within it every particle in this universe. If this were not the case, the absolute would not be unconditional, unqualified existence, since even a molecule that existed independently would exist in a loveless and separate universe. To be "absolute" means to contain absolutely everything and everybody— even those you consider to be "evil."

The relative is a fragmented view of life seen through the conditioned gross mind. Only the subtle mind can see the whole, unfragmented view of existence.

The relative is contained within the absolute just as the finger is contained within the hand, and the hand within the body. Because the gross mind sees the objects of the world as distinct and separate, it sees nationalities and races as distinct and separate. Therein lies the error of perception that has plagued the soul of humanity.

The Absolute and the relative are not different; they only exist as a different *perception* of one thing. We sometimes refer to that one thing as God, Tao, or Love.

LOVE

Life itself is the manifest shape of love. This includes every cell in your body, every thought in your mind, and every breath that you take. There is no escaping love; it is your very essence.

The gross mind loves only individual things and concepts; the subtle mind just loves.

Attention energy is the conveyance of love. By turning this energy inward, one can discover the profound silence that is divine love. In other words, one discovers one's true self.

Each cubic centimeter of space contains enough energy of love to support life eternally. Be still, breathe deeply, and let love permeate your heart.

The measurement of true love lies in our ability to love the world *as it is*, not necessarily the way we prefer it to be.

THE POWER OF ATTENTION

Without awareness there is no world to be seen. Awareness allows us to view the spectacle of life through the eyes of God.

No matter what kinds of illusions the gross mind creates, these instantly vanish when viewed through the divine power of attention.

Attention (focused awareness) turned outward creates this apparent world. When it is turned inward, we are able to perceive the eternal, unmanifest source of "what is."

By turning your vision inward, you will see that God has *always* been right here. Where else could the divine reside?

ETERNAL LIFE

True spiritual transformation liberates us from the limited life we know to the freedom of life eternal. Death of the physical body plays no part in this, for upon transformation we are no longer affected by the body's survival or demise.

Through the flowering of the subtle mind, we become transformed and live as divine, eternal Being. This is the true meaning of "God walking the earth."

When you awaken from the charade of the gross mind, you immediately realize that you were never anything other than eternal existence. Seeing this dispels fear once and for all.

Death is just a concept that relates to the duration of matter; it is a measurement used by the gross mind. The subtle mind knows only the immeasurable: life eternal.

Charade

Pointers on the Way

PART FOUR

"We shall not cease from exploration
And the end of all our exploring
Will be to arrive where we started
And know the place for the first time."
—T. S. ELIOT

Attention Exercises

*. . . an aspect of the mind practically unknown in the West that
seems obvious in the East, namely the self-liberating
power of the introverted mind.*
—From *The Tibetan Book of Great Liberation*, translation
by W. Y. Evans-Wenz, commentary by C. G. Jung

A fter the "word-erasing" experience I had in France, I clearly saw that any explanation of an experience will remain just that—an explanation. The word "water" will never quench your thirst, in the same way that the word "love" can never equal a simple hug.

Word symbols and the experiences they point to run parallel but can never meet. My goal has always been to share with others the *experience* of awakening from the illusory dreams I suffered from as a young boy to the peace and joy of the subtle mind. The following exercises do just that, and I offer them with love and gratitude.

ABOUT ATTENTION

Only when attention is removed from its obsession with thought can it operate with full power as a healing agent. The gross mind, because of its mechanical nature, will always respond to commands you give it, in the same way that applying the brakes will stop a car. The only difference is that, in this case, the energy of attention is the driver.

The benefits of these exercises are twofold: they help to resolve the problem of overactive thought, which in turn provides a sense of relative peace and calm. More importantly, they also give us the tools to move into the much greater space of pure awareness, the perspective from which apparent problems are still viewed but are no longer "owned" as one owns personal property. It is in this state that we truly awaken to the full implications of our humanity.

WHY THIS WORKS

The exercises in this book make use of the transformative power of awareness known as "attention," and their application calls for an introverted and intensified use of one's attentiveness. As Carl Jung has suggested, the introverted mind carries within it an inherent "self-liberating power." When the full power of attention is brought to bear, in a concentrated manner, it has the ability to bring the content of the mind into order. When thought is in order, a reality that is vast and timeless becomes available to us. This is sometimes called "Presence," "the Now," or "the Timeless State." I simply use the words "subtle mind."

How to Proceed

When earnestly applied, these Attention Exercises work consistently. Designed to be part of a twenty-one-week program, each exercise should last for ten minutes and is always preceded by the *Locating/Be Still* procedure, which lasts for five minutes. So the total time for each exercise is a full fifteen minutes. It is better not to focus much on the time or be overly concerned with it. In this spirit, go ahead and stay longer in each exercise if it feels right to you. It's important to do all of the exercises with your eyes open unless the application instructions state otherwise. The only exception to this is when you're using an exercise as a sleep aid.

Practice each exercise once every day for a period of six days (with one day off). In this manner, you'll complete all of the exercises in a twenty-one-week period. Please practice the exercises when you are rested and in the order in which they're presented.

The best way to carry out your daily practice is to *first* read through the specific exercise you are going to undertake that day in order to become familiar with it.

Toward the end of the first week—after completing the first exercise six times, and provided the exercise is practiced as prescribed—you may begin to feel a positive modification in consciousness. At the end of twenty-one weeks, you should feel a definite inward shift and taste the joy and freedom of the subtle mind.

Acknowledgement of Insights

When you're doing the Attention Exercises, it is *essential* that any new perceptions or insights be acknowledged by writing them down in a journal especially kept for this purpose. Your entries may be as long or as short as you like. For instance, if in the course of doing an exercise you get a sense of being inwardly empty and silent—as if the ego center no longer exists—you should write down this insight directly after the session. Writing down your insights will help to steady and deepen your progress.

The gross mind tends to release conditioning only when it is able to perceive a greater reality. Acknowledging these experiences in writing helps to solidify the quality of a specific insight. I call these written statements "insight notes" or "i-notes." One should keep these notes for reference at a later date. These i-notes, which describe new states of consciousness, will help to sustain the reality of those states.

An example of this was a student in one of my classes who, while in session, had a profound insight into the nature of her existence as pure beingness, followed by a period of deep inner peace. Several days later, she complained to me that she had "lost" that state. I asked that she acknowledge her insight and the experience of that peaceful state by writing it down, and to do the same for any insights she might have in the future. She did so, and thereafter, although the intensity of her experiences lessened, they still remained a significant influence in her everyday life.

A NATURAL RESTORATIVE

Several of these exercises are also ideal for helping to restore one's ability to sleep. When we begin to worry about a life situation, a rush of adrenaline often enters the bloodstream, acting as a stimulant. Once the mind becomes stimulated, it continues its heightened activity, creating even more thoughts and images, which in turn creates even more adrenaline. The exercises indicated with the ✳ symbol are very effective in stopping the torrent of thoughts and images. Once the appropriate exercise is applied, the mind is relieved of this condition and sleep occurs naturally.

After you have gone through all of the exercises (in order) at least once, you may find some of them to be especially effective under certain circumstances. Feel free to use the exercises that you feel are most effective for you. If there are no specific circumstances that are disturbing the mind, then just use the *Locate/Be Still* procedure, along with Exercise #1 (Holding the Head), on a daily basis.

Remember, the mind will always respond to whatever you tell it to do.

Always allow a full fifteen minutes for each session.

Start every session with the *Locate/Be Still* procedure for a period of five full minutes. This will ensure that the mind is brought back to the present moment.

It is important to drink a full glass of water several minutes before and after doing an exercise.

The *Locate/Be Still* procedure will ensure that you are not thinking, but *looking* (as attention) during each exercise.

The Exercises

PURPOSE

*This very powerful procedure helps you take your attention away
from the gross mind and into the quiet space of the subtle mind.
It plays an integral role in preparing the mind to be receptive
to the exercise that follows.*

ABOUT THIS EXERCISE

This is the primary exercise that you'll use throughout the program.
The *Locate/Be Still* procedure should be done just *before* beginning
any exercise. The sequence is very important and must be followed.
(The words *"Locate/Be Still"* are purposely set in italics to remind
you.)

Application

1. Take several deep breaths, then silently but emphatically say to
   yourself, *Slow down, slow down, be still!* Wait silently for several
   moments to allow the mind to become quiet.
2. Project your attention to a spot about two feet in front of your
   face. Without looking down, notice that you can see several parts
   of your body, such as arms and legs.
3. Notice that your peripheral vision has broadened to include the
   objects in the room. Open your peripheral vision still more widely
   and notice the adjacent walls. This is called "Open Attention."

4. Keeping your head still and with gentle Open Attention, slowly study the objects in the room. Include the object you call your body, which has now fallen into your field of vision.

5. Without turning your head become aware of the space behind your body.

6. Sit for five minutes with this effortless Open Attention, keeping your peripheral vision as widely open as possible. **Pay particular attention to how silent space is!**

This procedure helps restore the ability to feel love.

ABOUT THIS EXERCISE

This exercise disciplines the attention to remain focused, rather than allowing it to wander arbitrarily. At first, the attention may become distracted and begin to follow random thoughts. When this happens, just bring your attention back to the sensation of the head and hold it there. Over time, you'll be able to focus your attention wherever you want without the mind wandering. This process will very quickly tame the chattering mind.

Application

1. *Locate/Be Still.* Take several deep breaths and relax. Slow everything down.

2. Feel the weight of your head and put your full attention on it.

3. Consider your attention to be like the beam of a very powerful flashlight. From the *Locating* position (two feet in front of your face), aim the beam directly back at yourself and have it wrap itself lightly around your entire head.

4. If a thought arises, focus your attention in a more energetic concentration in order to stop its movement. If the thought moves, concentrate even more aggressively and move with it. Don't let it "get away."

5. When the thought movement stops, let up a bit on the concentration but remain alert, ready to repeat this procedure should another thought start to arise.

6. Under no circumstances should you get involved in the "story line" of the thought; simply observe it dispassionately.

7. Allow the silent space of this awareness to enter your body in the form of light. As the rays of light enter through the top of your head, feel every cell pulsating with light-energy.

8. As you feel your body filled with the light of pure attention, complete this exercise for the full duration. **Notice how silent the space is!**

Note: Sense how your body may feel like an empty shell.

PURPOSE

This procedure helps one to access the state of inner silence.

ABOUT THIS EXERCISE

This very effective yet simple technique was taught to me by a Buddhist monk who happened to be passing through New York City. He said that many monks use it before sitting in meditation for long hours. It quickly brings about great inner calm.

Application

1. *Locate/Be Still.* Take several deep breaths and relax. Slow everything down.
2. Using your index finger, press the center of your upper forehead firmly for five seconds.
3. Close your eyes and roll them back as though you were attempting to look at that same spot. Continue to keep your eyes closed and rolled back. If there is any strain, relax the eyes slightly.
4. Slowly and silently, begin to count backward, starting from the number thirty. As you count, allow about a three-second gap of silence between each number. Concentrate on the sound of your inner voice as you count. Visualize the numbers in your mind's eye and be aware of the silent gaps between each number.
5. You'll get to a point where your eyes will want to relax forward; let them do this. Stop counting and sit quietly for the remainder of the session. **Notice how silent the space is!**

This procedure restores the ability to discover truth.

ABOUT THIS EXERCISE

There is within every human being a calm, silent center of awareness that reflects all it sees but doesn't react to anything. It is like a bright, shining mirror; it is pure consciousness. When you look at the world as a silent mirror, you become tranquil, inwardly silent, and unflappable. This exercise helps to get you there.

As you look out on the world, in your relationships with people, be a mirror. Just reflect all that you see. That is all. Do nothing, just reflect. Be a mirror that even reflects your own thoughts.

Application

1. *Locate/Be Still.* Take several deep breaths and relax. Slow everything down.
2. Go to a room in which there's a medium-size mirror. Stand in front of the mirror, but off to one side so that you can see part of the room but no part of your body.
3. Notice how the mirror only reflects, and that it never changes anything on its own. It silently and passively remains the unmoved witness.
4. Continue this silent watching for about two minutes. Be aware of the sound of your breathing and the silent space around you.
5. Slowly step in front of the mirror and gently notice your body. See how the mirror reflects your movement but still remains a

passive witness. Make some movements with your hands and notice how the mirror does nothing but reflect. This is an exact reflection of "what is."

6. Sit down in a comfortable chair and notice your body. For the remainder of the session, *mirror what you see.*

7. You may close your eyes and remain silent, but always remember to be a passive mirror. **Notice how silent the space is!**

This procedure reestablishes a calm mind.

ABOUT THIS EXERCISE

Very rarely is the quality of silence present in the mind. Thoughts come and go, usually one overlapping the other so there's no room for silence between them.

The scenario may go something like this: For some reason you think of your Aunt Helen, which then reminds you of your cousin Bob; but the thought about your cousin Bob generally overlaps your thought about Aunt Helen. A few moments later you think about your cousin Bob's wife and the fact that she works for a law firm; this thought gives birth to an overlapping thought about your own attorney, who is with the same firm, quickly followed by another overlapping thought reminding you about a pending legal issue. The thought of the pending legal matter brings about real fear, which is followed by an overlapping thought concerning your company's tax situation—this carries with it a big surge of adrenaline.

On and on and on it goes, one thought overlapping another. Where is there any room for silence? It's enough to drive one mad. It seems this scenario is the condition of the average mind, which is almost like a madhouse. Is there any escape? Any way to get out of this circle of thoughts? Unlike some societies in the East, Western society doesn't allow us the time to sit each day in long periods of meditation. Yet we desperately want to find the calm, silent mind.

Let us see if in fact there really is a silent place in the mind—see whether it exists at all—by bringing thought to a logical completion. An example of this would be: *I'm going to phone Aunt Helen tonight for her birthday.* This is the completion of a logical thought. Another example might be, *Aunt Helen is in Florida on a vacation; I'm going to have dinner with her when she comes back.* This is another example of logically completed thought.

When a thought is complete, allow a little space between that thought and the beginning of the next—if only for a second or two. The next thought that occurs to you might be: *I'd better make an appointment with my dentist before I go on vacation.* The key to this exercise is to allow space between this thought and the next one! We don't want the two thoughts to overlap; always allow a few moments' gap between them.

By living in "the gap between thoughts," you will notice the silence that naturally exists within this gap. It's as though a curtain has parted that was keeping you from experiencing the ever-present silence behind it. As you continue to do this exercise daily, the gaps between the thoughts will become longer and you'll experience a silence that's truly refreshing and energizing . . . the silence of the mind at rest.

Application
1. *Locate/Be Still.* Take several deep breaths and relax. Slow everything down.
2. Begin to watch your thoughts, allowing random ones to arise.
3. Don't try to stop thought, but allow each thought to come to its logical completion. Say silently to yourself, "Stop," in order to prevent a new thought from overlapping the existing one.
4. Don't allow your thoughts to overlap one another.

5. Allow about a four-second silent gap to occur between thoughts. Note the quality of the silence within this gap.
6. Continue this exercise for a full ten minutes, following the above procedure.
7. Relax and sit quietly for as long as you like. **Notice how silent the space is!**

Note: The next time you do this exercise, allow the silent gap to remain open for eight seconds.

For the purpose of this exercise, here are five statements you can use to open the gap between thoughts. Use these one after another and you'll see how thought can automatically subside. Then, in your everyday circumstances, simply apply this same technique to the random thoughts that normally arise.

Silently say to yourself:

My name is (your name) . . . Stop!
My mother's name is (mother's name) . . . Stop!
My father's name is (father's name) . . . Stop!
I live in (name of country) . . . Stop!
I am a (woman or man) . . . Stop!

Exercise 5
WATCHING THE MONKEY

PURPOSE
This procedure helps to bring inner calm amid outer chaos.

ABOUT THIS EXERCISE

Watching the Monkey can be done at any time, anywhere. It is best done when you're with a group of people in either a business or social situation in which, if you're honest, you can see yourself playing many roles: "the winner," "wanting approval," "the need to control," "the desire to dominate"—or having feelings of envy, jealousy, anger, or even boredom.

We sometimes go along with the group in order to shine, appear witty, or do whatever it takes to gain approval or avoid the disapproval of others in the group. For example: Someone makes a critical remark about another and we immediately join in with our bit of critical gossip. Or someone brings up a subject and we try desperately to think of a joke, idea, or statement that will top the precious contribution. Our mad monkey mind is always trying desperately to stay in the game—to be one of the group no matter what.

The purpose of this exercise is to just "watch the monkey." Observe the monkey mind in this manner: There's the "funny monkey," trying to be humorous in order to give the group a good laugh and gain their approval; the "gossip monkey," joining in gossip, putting down a mutual friend, and having a laugh at the expense of someone who's not there to defend himself; the "show-off monkey," telling everyone how she accomplished something and did it better than anyone else. Then there's the "annoyed monkey": a fellow worker just made a cutting remark about a project you worked on; just watch the monkey getting angry. There's the "embarrassed monkey"—painfully embarrassed about some silly remark he just made to the boss; the "self-loathing monkey": *Why did I say that, why was I such a showoff?* or *Why was I such a gossip? Why did I put my friend Sam down just to be amusing?*

This exercise is designed to help you end all the various roles that the monkey plays. You're not going to try to stop the monkey. Rather, you are going to watch it and identify what the monkey is saying or doing. When a certain thought comes into your mind, such as *Oh, I know a better joke* or *I'll tell them the one about the man at the bar with the dog*, all you have to do is silently notice what it is you're about to do. The idea is to identify the monkey behavior, then silently verbalize it by stating *Showing off*, and just quietly watch. Don't try to stop the thought, just notice it, identify it, and silently verbalize its characteristic. Next, watch the thought as it fades.

Finally, stop any silent dialogue and just watch your inner thoughts quietly. You'll see your mind become very silent. If you're being critical, just say, *Bob, you're being critical*, then watch silently. You'll notice that the desire to loudly verbalize the critical thought will have vanished, and your mind will be still. Alternatively, you can silently identify this characteristic by just naming it, e.g., *Jealous, Angry, Embarrassed*, or whatever you see the monkey dramatizing.

The principle of this exercise is to *catch* the monkey. Once caught, it is exposed, and it slips away. Eventually, the monkey may vanish completely.

Application

1. *Locate/Be Still.* Take several deep breaths and relax. Slow everything down.
2. This exercise is best done in a group. Become aware of your thoughts as you speak, or just watch the people in the group.
3. Silently notice any of your own compulsive reactions to what is occurring, whether it is seeking approval, trying to control or dominate, going along with group gossip, looking to shine, feeling jealous or envious, or trying to be witty.
4. Notice your mental attitude. When you feel you're about to act out any of the above compulsions, verbalize it to yourself silently. For example, if you feel the need for approval, watch the "approval monkey" and silently say, *Bob, you want approval.* Immediately stop and watch in silence. Or, if you feel critical, watch the "critical monkey" and silently say, *Mary, you're being critical.* **Immediately stop and watch in silence.**

EXERCISE 5 - PART TWO
WATCHING THE MONKEY IN OTHERS

This variation of the previous exercise helps you to spot "the monkey" in others. Look around the room and see if you can notice what their inner monkey is saying, doing, or chattering about. You will see it very quickly. You will also notice that if you watch silently, your own monkey mind will disappear.

Application

1. Sometime, start to notice the game or games that the other monkeys (other people's minds) are playing.
2. Note their monkeys in silence, and notice that their bodies and yours exist in the same quiet space. **Notice how silent the space is!**

Purpose

This procedure allows one to overcome anxiety.

About This Exercise

Depressed, anxious, blue, feeling down, under the weather. We often hear these terms and probably use them ourselves. But what exactly is the *sensation* of being depressed, a feeling that can be so unpleasant that it makes living nearly impossible?

The feelings of depression or conflict produce a sense of heaviness somewhere in the body. One usually feels a sensation of pressing heaviness somewhere in the chest, in the abdomen, or even in the throat or shoulders.

What if these physical sensations were not there? Would we still feel depressed? Many people use alcohol or drugs to obtain temporary relief from this heaviness. I recommend avoiding drugs or alcohol, as these only constrain our ability to solve the problem.

The solution we want is to get rid of any unpleasant physical sensations while continuing to search for the *source* of these feelings. This particular exercise, "Hugging the Heaviness," does just that. It quickly relieves the heavy physical feeling associated with depression or the blues. It is now a well-known fact that when these physical sensations are no longer present in the body, the psychological depression may also dissipate.

Application

1. *Locate/Be Still.* Take several deep breaths and relax. Slow everything down.

2. Mentally look around your body to see if you can locate a heavy feeling or pressure sensation that may be associated with a current source of anxiety, or even with an old, unresolved conflict.

3. Once you locate this sensation, put all your attention fully on it. Really concentrate your attention on the heavy feeling, hugging it tightly with your awareness so that there's no space between your hugging and the sensation of heaviness. You'll need to hug very tightly until the sensation becomes transparent.

4. Slowly ease off on the hugging and see if any of the heavy sensation still remains. If any does, put your attention on it again and hug very tightly for about ten seconds. Let up and again check to see if any of the heaviness is still there. Continue the hugging procedure until none of the heavy feeling remains.

5. Relax for a few moments, look around, and see if there are any other heavy sensations in your body. If you find one, hug it while repeating the entire procedure.

6. Do this exercise for a full ten minutes, increasing the time if necessary. **Notice how silent the space is!**

Exercise 7
HUGGING YOUR HEAD

PURPOSE
This procedure restores one's natural state of tranquility.

ABOUT THIS EXERCISE
Sometimes we have a sensation of heaviness that's located mostly in the head. It's not as though we had a headache, although there may be a slight headachy feeling. This procedure, called "Hugging Your Head," is meant to relieve this heaviness.

Application
1. *Locate/Be Still.* Take several deep breaths and relax. Slow everything down.
2. Find the sensation of heaviness in your head. Really feel the weight of your head and your neck. Put the full power of your attention on your head.
3. Hug so tightly with your attention energy that there is no space between your hugging and the sensation of heaviness. Continue hugging until you feel that your head has become lighter, almost transparent.
4. Direct your attention to the inside of your head and move in as if you were slowly entering the interior of your skull. Look around, stay there for a few moments, then move out of the other side of your head. Stay there for a few seconds, continuing to hug your head very tightly.
5. Continue this procedure until you feel that your head is almost completely transparent or weightless.

6. Sit and relax for several minutes in silence. If any heaviness recurs, begin to hug your head again, hugging very tightly until the silence returns. Sit and silently notice that your arms and legs are occupying space. **Notice how silent the space is!**

Exercise 8
REMOVING STRESS ENERGY #1:
FROM THE TORSO AND LIMBS

Purpose
This procedure alleviates feelings of anxiety by removing stress energy from the body.

About This Exercise
Stress energy (SE) gets stored on the physical level in certain areas of the body. It's possible to remove SE from these areas through the power of focused attention, which can burn stress energy in the same way that the sun, when focused through a magnifying glass, can burn dry paper.

These areas that contain SE are generally the result of past upsets, when the chaotic mental energy flow from the upset was suppressed rather than released. This energy can store itself in the body for years and may play a part in causing present upsets and illness. This exercise can help to release some of the negative effects of stress energy.

Application
1. *Locate/Be Still.* Take several deep breaths and relax. Slow everything down.
2. Look around your body and find an area of denseness similar to the sensation you feel in the body when upset.
3. Direct a focused stream of attention to the area of denseness. When you feel a release of energy and a venting occurs, the stress energy has been released.

4. Wait about five seconds, then look for other areas of density in your body and repeat this procedure.

5. This exercise may be used at any time during normal daily activities when you experience a buildup of stress energy and wish to release it. **Always notice how silent the space is!**

REMOVING STRESS ENERGY #2:
FROM THE HEAD

PURPOSE
This procedure restores the ability to feel at ease by removing stress energy from the head.

ABOUT THIS EXERCISE
This exercise is based on the techniques used in Exercise 8. We'll use the same procedure, but in this case stress energy (SE) is to be removed from the head.

Application
1. *Locate/Be Still.* Take several deep breaths and relax. Slow everything down.
2. Be aware of your head region, look around there, and find an area of denseness similar to the sensation you feel in your body when upset.
3. Direct a focused stream of attention to the area of denseness. When you feel a release of energy and a venting occurs, the SE has been released.
4. Wait about five seconds, then look for other areas of denseness in your head, repeating this procedure if necessary.
5. This exercise may be used at any time during normal daily activities when you experience a buildup of stress energy in your head. **Always notice how silent the space is!**

Exercise 10
AUTO-REMOVAL OF STRESS ENERGY

PURPOSE
This procedure brings back the ability to experience awe & wonderment.

ABOUT THIS EXERCISE
This exercise should be done *only* after completing Exercises 8 and 9. It is meant to set into motion the reflexive removal of stress energy, especially when one is involved in a tense or anxious situation. Auto-Removal will ensure that SE is being removed during highly stressful moments. It is also very effective during your busy daily activities when you may be too occupied to initiate a formal session. The Auto-Removal exercise requires about one minute to be set into play.

Application
1. *Locate/Be Still.* Take several deep breaths and relax. Slow everything down.
2. Hold your right thumb to your forefinger and press firmly. Next, apply a focused stream of attention on the two joined fingers.
3. Silently say, *Auto-Remove.*
4. Each time you join those fingers, a small amount of attention will search out SE automatically, even when you're busy with other things.
5. You'll know when there is a removal because of the venting sensation.
6. When you wish to end Auto Remove, place your left thumb and forefinger together and silently say with conviction, *End Auto-Remove.* **Notice how silent the space is!**

Exercise 11
GETTING TOUGH

PURPOSE
This procedure gives you the ability to stay in control of your reactive mind.

ABOUT THIS EXERCISE

When you find yourself tense, agitated, or overwhelmed because you're unable to get on with the job at hand, it's often because the mad monkey is raging within you. Using the Getting Tough exercise will restore you to a naturally calm condition.

Whenever you begin to feel impatient, agitated, anxious, or upset, notice your condition, then say silently but firmly to yourself, *Be quiet. Calm down, Mary* (use your name here), *just calm down!* Say this with great authority. If you have the opportunity to say it aloud (even under your breath), it works even better.

The words chosen should be yours, of course, but there must be great intention and authority behind the words. If any further agitation arises, get tough with the monkey again.

Note: The mind will always respond to whatever you tell it to do.

Application
1. *Locate/Be Still.* Take several deep breaths and relax. Slow everything down.
2. Focus your attention on the source of your breath.
3. With a high degree of intention, shout silently to yourself, telling your monkey mind to *Stop right now! Calm down! Be still!*

4. Silently notice all mental activity and slow everything down.
5. If there are no other people around, speak the commands out loud. **Then notice how silent the space is!**

Exercise 12*
SLOWING IT DOWN

PURPOSE
This procedure provides you with the ability to expand your consciousness and release impatience.

ABOUT THIS EXERCISE
At times, our natural state of calmness suddenly deserts us. We experience a feeling of impatience, yet what we're doing at that moment really requires patience. As a result, we're unable to properly concentrate on the business at hand.

When you feel rushed, overwhelmed, or impatient, silently notice the impatient condition. Don't judge it or be critical; simply notice your own state of being impatient.

Application
1. *Locate/Be Still.* Take several deep breaths and relax. Slow everything down.
2. Focus your attention on the source of your breath.
3. Silently or aloud, depending on your surroundings, state to yourself in a slow and forceful manner, *Slow it down! Slow down, Ron* (use your name here). *Just slow everything down. Be calm.*
4. Follow this procedure again until you notice that your mind fully complies, releases the impatience, and becomes relaxed. **Notice how silent the space is!**

This procedure restores the ability to experience inner peace and feel one's connection to others.

ABOUT THIS EXERCISE

Rarely can a person look around and identify what he or she sees. I'm not speaking about a room full of hundreds of objects, but one that might contain only ten or fifteen items. The key idea is to look around the room and note what you see. Why is it that almost everyone leaves something out?

What people leave out is the *space* right in front of them. I call this phenomenon "Space Blindness." And, although it may seem like an insignificant omission, it happens to be one of the most critical errors the human mind has ever made. It is this omission that leads to feelings of isolation, alienation, and imprisonment. Einstein called this " . . . a kind of optical delusion of one's consciousness." It is this very feeling that leads to conflict between people and, ultimately, nations.

In the following exercise, we will reconsider whether space separates us or connects us to one another.

Application

1. *Locate/Be Still.* Take several deep breaths and relax. Slow everything down.

2. Slowly and silently notice that your body is sitting in a chair that is located in space along with all of the other objects in the

room. Observe your arms and legs and see how they occupy the space in front of you.

3. Notice that the same space in which your body appears extends out into the entire physical universe. This space contains your body, the room, the building you're in, the city and country in which you live, and the entire planet as well.

4. Bring your attention back into the room in which you're sitting and notice how the space is actually *connecting* you to the other objects in the room.

5. Be very aware of the space, even more than the objects in it. It's almost as if you're sitting in "space soup." Really concentrate on the space so that you become aware of the expanse in which all of the objects reside.

6. Get a feeling of the space behind you and on all sides. If there's a window available, look out and notice the space out there too.

7. If a thought arises, note the space again, and see that even this thought exists in the same space as your body, and that it is nothing more than an object in space. **Notice how silent the space is!**

Exercise 14
INCLUDING THE SEER IN THE SEEING

PURPOSE

This procedure enables the mind to awaken to ever-present awareness.

ABOUT THIS EXERCISE

As we look out at the world, we often feel separate, isolated, and alone. It's as if we have been looking out from a shadowy closet within the mind for most of our life, when all the while we've been surrounded by the immeasurable presence that is here and now. We generally don't realize that we wound up in this false reality solely through the conditioning of the mind. With this exercise, we can begin to get a truer perception of "where" we really are.

Application

1. *Locate/Be Still.* Take several deep breaths and relax. Slow everything down.
2. Look around and silently notice your arms and legs as you sit in the chair. Carefully study them and see how they exist along with the other objects in the space of the room.
3. While keeping your full attention on a part of your body, widen your peripheral view to include the walls of the room. Continue to hold this wide view while silently noticing the other objects in the room, which now include part of your body. Your concentration should be only on your body and the other objects in the room.

4. Really see how you *occupy the same space* as the other objects in the room. In the seeing, it is essential to include a part of your body at all times.
5. If a thought suddenly distracts your attention, bring it right to your body and the space around it.
6. Stay in the space you're in right now. Don't move back into the "closet." Even if thoughts float back, remain aware that your body occupies the immediate space of *here and now*. Thoughts will end and your mind will be tranquil and silent. **Notice how silent the space is!**

Note: No matter what your activity may be, always try to include the seer in the seeing.

Exercise 15
ASKING CONSCIOUSNESS

PURPOSE

This procedure restores your ability to feel inner peace and aids you in gaining a new perspective on problems that arise in your relations with others.

ABOUT THIS EXERCISE

The mind is excellent for solving technical problems. If we get enough facts, put them together, and run them through the computer located just above our neck, we can usually come up with a decent solution. However, the problems and conflicts that arise between people are not so easily solved by this same apparatus.

Like a computer, the mind contains all of the past programs that have been placed there to solve certain problems. Because of this, the mind is often incapable of solving problems that fall outside its range of preprogrammed solutions. This exercise lets us bypass this facility to see if there is another source that might, when addressed, shed new light on an old problem.

Application
1. *Locate/Be Still.* Take several deep breaths and relax. Slow everything down.
2. Ask yourself a serious question, perhaps one that concerns a problem you've been recently facing. It might be a question such as *How can I improve my relationship with my boss?* or *What is it that my children expect of me?* It's important that it be a problem that really concerns you.

3. Don't accept answers that come from the gross mind (the "old program"). Just wait silently, with the firm conviction that you will not accept any answer based in thoughts or ideas. If thought offers an answer, disregard it. Just let thoughts come and go.

4. If you see the problem from the perspective of the subtle mind, you may realize that there's not much depth to it—in spite of how the gross mind carried on when you were under its influence.

5. If you continue waiting, a deep silence will come to you that will carry the answer to your question. This is a silence that comes from asking a question but *not allowing the gross mind to answer*. The answer may come in a completely different manner than you expected. It will, however, be a *living* solution—not another idea or concept.

6. Stay in this silence; the question that you asked is being heard at a profound level of your consciousness. Your question *will* be answered. **Notice how silent the space is!**

Exercise 16
HAVING OBJECTS LOOK AT YOU

PURPOSE
This procedure reestablishes one's ability to love the world.

ABOUT THIS EXERCISE

All people see themselves at the center of life, something like the sun around which all planets revolve. This may be due to the fact that human consciousness is basically self-centered by nature. From the moment a child becomes self-aware (*I am "me"*), he or she becomes a fixed physical and psychological center around which all life revolves. For the rest of their lives, people are conditioned to see the world from that center, feeling it to be the most important center of all.

This exercise helps bring about a new perception concerning the true nature of subject-object relationships. It dispels the illusion of a self-centered existence and may also expand your perception to the degree that you will never again see yourself as having a "fixed" center.

Application

1. *Locate/Be Still.* Take several deep breaths and relax. Slow everything down.
2. Look at an object in the room, such as a cup, a book, or a vase.
3. Really look at the object and feel the flow of awareness going from you to the object. Do this for about one minute.
4. Now reverse the process. Feel that the object is now aware of you, and that its awareness is flowing toward you. Reinforce the

idea that the cup has become *aware* of you, and that it is flowing its attention toward you.

5. Now, *you are the object and it is the subject*, and it knows that you are there.
6. Next, have all of the other objects in the room flow their awareness toward you. They are looking at you, and the flow of energy going on between all the objects includes you.
7. Return to the cup and have it fix its attention on you. Just feel and accept its flow of energy coming toward you. Silently notice how even *space is aware of you.*
8. Sit quietly, feeling the flow from the cup, for the balance of the session. **Notice how silent the space is!**

Exercise 17
CUTTING OFF THE HEAD

PURPOSE

This procedure imparts the ability to experience inner space.

ABOUT THIS EXERCISE

In this exercise, we use a laser-like saber to mentally cut off one's own head in order to perceive life from a center not based in the world of mental images and ideas. By keeping your attention on the space that your head previously occupied, you may experience the truly unlimited nature of awareness.

Application

1. *Locate/Be Still.* Take several deep breaths and relax. Slow everything down.

2. Imagine that you have just cut off your head, using a sharp, laser-like saber. It was completely painless and very quiet. Now there is only space where your head used to be.

3. Looking out from the empty space where your head once was, carefully observe all of the objects in the room, including your body.

4. Stay seated for the full duration of this exercise, and see what the perception of the world might be for a "headless" person.

5. If a thought happens to come into the empty space, cut off your head again and continue to sit in the quiet, open space of awareness. **Notice how silent the space is!**

Exercise 18*
WATCHING THE WATCHER

PURPOSE
This procedure bestows the ability to remain mindful.

ABOUT THIS EXERCISE

Several Eastern meditative traditions speak of the "witness" or "watcher," which observes the thought-based habits of the meditator for the purpose of bringing mental activities to an end. One of the problems with this approach is that we can easily fall into the trap of letting the gross mind play the role of the witness. This is something like having a thief walking around, disguised as a policeman and assuring everyone that he'll guard against all thievery.

There truly is an impartial observer that can prevent the thieving mind from robbing you of inner peace and precious mental energy. But how do we tell the difference between the real witness and the counterfeit? In witnessing, you'll notice that the counterfeit observer generally articulates on what it's watching, whereas the real witness will always watch silently. Therefore, if you hear any kind of articulation, comment, or judgment about anything at all, you'll know that you're hearing from the imposter witness—the monkey in disguise.

If you try to silence the chattering and find it getting worse, call on the genuine witness to silently watch the counterfeit one. When the real watcher observes, the monkey mind will immediately become silent.

Note: The *Locate/Be Still* procedure serves to silence the imposter witness and should be used whenever you find it difficult to quiet some mental chatter.

Application

1. *Locate/Be Still.* Take several deep breaths and relax. Slow everything down.

2. Silently notice that your body occupies the same space as all of the other objects in the room. Remember to *include the seer in the seeing.* Actually see your arms and legs in the seeing.

3. Watch any thoughts that come into your mind, whether they're random or specific. Simply be aware of thoughts and see how they come and go. This is their nature.

4. You may see that the observer of these thoughts is still part of the mental process. In other words, this is still a case of the mind watching the mind. Let this continue in this manner for about half a minute.

5. Now, silently observe the entire mental process, which includes thoughts *and the watcher of these thoughts,* from a location just behind your body.

6. From this shifted perspective, silently observe the watcher of thoughts. If the so-called observer comments on or gets involved with the content of any thought, silently observe this without interfering.

7. You are the pure witness of all that happens in the mind. You witness only, and never get involved in any way with what is being witnessed. Remain silent, observing the entire mental process.

8. From the same (shifted) location, somewhere behind your body,

begin to watch the random thoughts as they come into your mind. Do this for about half a minute.

9. From this same position, become silently aware of the entire mental process, which now includes the thoughts and the watcher of the thoughts. Do this for the full duration of the session.

10. If thoughts arise silently, observe the false watcher of thoughts with patience and care. **Always notice how silent the space is!**

Exercise 19
SEARCHING FOR THE THINKER

This procedure allows the attention to remain awake in the present.

ABOUT THIS EXERCISE

If you ask most people who they are, they'll generally say, "Why, I'm me." And if you ask, "Where is this me?" they'll generally point to their body. If questioned further, they usually agree that they are not the body itself, but something within the body. When asked how they know this, they often say, "Because I hear myself talking and thinking. This is how I know that I am, and where I am."

This exercise will help you to settle this question once and for all—not as an idea or philosophy but as an actual perception.

Application

1. *Locate/Be Still.* Take several deep breaths and relax. Slow everything down.

2. Allow random everyday thoughts to arise, and see if you can locate the *thinker* of these thoughts.

3. Using your attention, move right into the place in your body where you feel the thinker—the source of thoughts—is located, and see if you can find "him." Search with lots of energy, as though you were trying to find something you had lost. Look really hard.

4. After a few minutes of searching, consider whether there is a thinker at all—or is it just *the process of thinking* that has created an illusory thinker?

5. Ask yourself if it is at all possible to find the source of thoughts, but don't mentally answer!

6. Sit in silence for the duration of the exercise. If any thoughts arise during this time, try to find the thinker behind these thoughts. **Notice how silent the space is!**

Exercise 20
SILENT LISTENING/SILENT SPEECH

Purpose
This procedure restores the ability to experience love.

About This Exercise

So many problems arise due to the fact that people don't know how to truly listen. They often say, "Yes, I hear you," yet they are not really listening to you, but to their own thoughts. In fact, mentally they are often busy rehearsing their response. If they truly heard you, the interaction would take place at a much deeper level of communication.

Is it really possible to fully listen to someone who is speaking to you? This would require you to listen to another without listening to your own thoughts at that moment. In other words, to truly *hear* what the other person means, you would have to listen with a mind that is silent.

This exercise is designed to help you listen with a silent, passive mind, no matter what is being said. As a result, you'll gain a deeper understanding of the speaker and his or her true intention.

Application

1. *Locate/Be Still.* Take several deep breaths and relax. Slow everything down.
2. Hug your head, using the full power of your attention. Feel the weight and mass of your head while hugging it.

3. Slowly move your attention into the interior of your head and silently look around inside your skull. Now slowly move out the other side.

4. Hug your head again, really tightly. Now move into the interior of your head and stay there for a few moments before moving out the other side.

5. Silently locate the center of your consciousness, and when you do, fall deeply into it. Stay in the deep, infinite space, which is quiet and calm. Remain there for the duration of the session until the silence is stabilized.

6. Listen to any sounds that come out of the surrounding environment from this deep, deep quietude. Let the sounds approach you and tumble into the profound silence.

7. In this state of silence, slowly get up and leave the room, making sure that you're fully aware of your movements.

8. Slow everything down. Silently notice your arms and legs moving in space. If any thoughts arise, don't resist them. Just tightly hug your head again until the silence returns.

9. Walk around the environment you're in, going outdoors if you prefer. Look for people to talk to. Listen *passively*, from the deep silence, to what they say, and if a response is necessary, speak it from the same deep silence.

10. Keep everything slowed down and very casual. Continue like this for thirty minutes. If there are no other people to speak with, then listen to the sounds of the environment from deep, deep within your Being. **Notice how silent the space is!**

Note: Work with this exercise until you understand the nature of *passive* listening, which is derived from deep silence.

This procedure allows one to perceive life as one consciousness.

ABOUT THIS EXERCISE

Ordinarily, you experience yourself as a separate, isolated individual. You have a feeling that, like the sun, you're a distinct center around which everything in the world revolves. You're the main character, while others merely play supporting roles in the drama called "my life." This feeling of being the central character in life has a distinct "flavor" to it.

Only when you clearly recognize that all other persons in the world also experience themselves as the central character, and see you and others as only bit players, you may suddenly realize there is just one consciousness playing different roles.

When this phenomenon is experienced, the *assumed* differences between yourself and others will fade away, and the recognition of a mutually shared consciousness will become your primary sense of being. You may then live in the world while identifying with this one consciousness.

Note: This exercise is to be done at a restaurant or any other quiet public place. Work with this exercise until you recognize the distinct feeling of individuation that always exists within you.

Application

1. *Locate/Be Still.* Take several deep breaths and relax. Slow everything down.

2. Turn your attention inward until you feel the quality of your individual beingness. Hold this feeling for several minutes.

3. While continuing to hold your feeling of individual beingness, look outward and notice the other people around you. Understand that everyone you see also experiences himself or herself, in this very moment, in an identical manner.

4. You may notice now that the former feeling of difference between you and everyone else has disappeared, and in its place is a profound sense of *one consciousness* that is uniting everyone.

5. As you continue to hold this experience, you'll see that everyone is actually unified as the one consciousness.

6. Remain with this feeling for the rest of the session. **Always notice the silent space in which all objects exist!**

In Conclusion

Now that you've spent time with these exercises, you will have discovered that the gross mind can be quieted through the power of attention. You'll want to be on guard during periods of low energy, because when you're tired you may not have sufficient energy to handle mental fluctuations.

The basic principle to recognize is that any deviation in mental behavior should immediately alert one to the play of the gross mind. When this happens, allow plenty of open space where there is no room for thought to hide. Allow thought to take its course, but witness it diligently, and it will fade away. The more you live in this manner, the longer you'll be able to remain in the calm, silent space of the subtle mind, which is always present and fully awake.

BEING A BUDDHA ON BROADWAY

Afterword

Sometime toward the end of Jeannie's and my stay in France, we got a telephone call from a photographer friend who lived in a nearby village. He said he wanted to stop by to show our house to a visiting friend and his wife. Our friend went on to say that his guest was the famous architect I. M. Pei, who was in France to attend a state dinner. The dinner was to honor him for having designed the magnificent glass pyramid that occupies the courtyard of the Louvre museum in Paris.

After Pei and his wife arrived, I gave them a tour of the house. When we reached my studio in the attic, I. M. sat down in the meditation chair, from where he could view most of the village. I told him that I used the studio to paint, and that I was presently writing a book on meditation. He remarked that the room had an extraordinary silence, and that he was interested in meditation.

Suddenly his eyes fixed on a note that I had earlier pinned to a low-hanging beam. The note articulated an important Zen attitude:

"No grasping." When Pei, who is Chinese-American, read these words, a broad smile appeared on his face. He remarked, "Now I know why I visited you." He went on to explain that for the past few days he had been wondering what the proper response should be to the great honor the French nation was about to bestow on him. Now, he said, my note had just conveyed to him what the appropriate response should be: "No grasping."

There are many similar "notes" within this book. My profound wish is that, like I. M. Pei, readers may find the exact one that they have been searching for—one that has the potential to reveal their own "proper response" to the sacred presence permeating their life.

ABOUT SUBTLEMIND.COM

SubtleMind.com is the Internet home of author and Academy-Award winning director B. W. Salzman and the Subtle Mind method. At SubtleMind.com you may leave your comments about *Being a Buddha on Broadway*, or find out about Bert Salzman's speaking engagements.

SubtleMind.com

ABOUT INNER DIRECTIONS

InnerDirections Publishing is the imprint of the Inner Directions Foundation, a nonprofit organization dedicated to exploring self-discovery and awakening to one's essential nature, in the spirit of nonduality.

We produce and publish distinctive books, videos, and audiotapes that reflect the heart of authentic spirituality. These highly regarded works present clear and direct approaches to realizing *That* which is eternal and infinite within us—the source from which religions and spiritual traditions arise.

We depend upon the support of people like you—friends who recognize the merit of an organization whose sole purpose is to disseminate works of enduring spiritual value. To receive our catalog or to find out how you can help sponsor an upcoming publishing project, call, write, or e-mail:

Inner Directions
P. O. Box 130070
Carlsbad, CA 92013

Tel: 760 599-4075
Fax: 760 599-4076
Orders: 800 545-9118

E-mail: mail@InnerDirections.org
Website: www.InnerDirections.org